THE LADY

THE LADY

STUDIES OF CERTAIN SIGNIFICANT
PHASES OF HER HISTORY

BY

EMILY JAMES PUTNAM

WITH A FOREWORD BY

JEANNETTE MIRSKY

THE UNIVERSITY OF CHICAGO PRESS

CHICAGO & LONDON

SBN: 226-68562-4 (clothbound); 226-68564-0 (paperbound)
Library of Congress Catalog Card Number: 70-108990

The University of Chicago Press, Chicago 60637
The University of Chicago Press, Ltd., London

Originally published by G. P. Putnam's Sons
Copyright 1910 by Emily James Putnam; copyright
renewed 1938 by Emily James Putnam
Foreword © 1969 by
The University of Chicago. All rights reserved

This edition published 1970
Printed in the United States of America

CONTENTS

FOREWORD

Emily James Putnam was Barnard College's first dean; she came back in 1914 and, until her retirement in 1929, lectured on Greek literature in translation. I took the two courses she gave. Those of us who had the good fortune to know her as a teacher remember how bravely we awaited her first appearance in the classroom. Rumors had warned us: she would permit no nonsense; she expected close attention in class and diligent, thorough preparation. Her courses were rated "tough" and so were the marks she gave. Curious, expectant, we awaited her entrance, chatting in spurts, our manner subdued. She entered quietly, looked around the room, bade us "good morning" and, with no further remarks, handed out her reading list. It was lengthy and formidable.

All the warnings were quickly forgotten. Through the reading we did, she made us her partners in an exciting adventure; everything came alive and had meaning. Hers was a kind of setting-up exercise for the muscles of our intelligence, making the experiences and sensibilities of long-dead writers loom larger than our raw set of beliefs. Her lectures, presented in casual but polished prose, were handsomely funded by her rich knowledge of European literature. Together we reconnoitered, ranging and zigzagging through the works of Greek, Roman, English, French, Spanish, Italian, and German writers while following a theme or a literary form, made conscious of subtle changes in the various manifestations. Her lectures were dazzling: her wit suggested detachment and her wisdom offered the freedom to choose one's prejudices for oneself; these qualities were happily joined to sensitivity and a clean, firm judgment. She was free of pretensions and disdained oversimplifications, obfuscations and facile opinions. Questions and discussion were encouraged. Fully aware of how little we knew, without condescending, she placed her erudition within our grasp.

Her appearance and manner set her apart from the other women on the faculty. At the time I took her courses she was in her early sixties. Her slight figure had fleshed out, but she still walked lightly and moved gracefully. Her hair, once a pale blonde, frizzed and coiffed, was crowned with a tocque in the manner of her contemporary, the late Queen Mary. I remember a georgette blouse that she wore (puce the color was then called; today it is eggplant) brightened by a fine gold chain on which she carried her lorgnette. This she held to her eyes while reading aloud and then, when making a comment, she used it as a symphony conductor's baton to signal a passage. An Edwardian? Perhaps. She had that period's charm and elegance and delight in small, wholly personal fancies; but she had none of its affectations and languor, its fussiness and hauteur. Remembering has made me conscious that she fascinated us as a woman as well as a teacher.

Remembering her vividly after so long a time, I realized that I knew nothing about her background and development. Seeking answers, I began to understand what had formed her and how she had formed herself.

Emily James Smith (1865–1944) was born in Canandaigua, a comfortable farming community in the fertile, rolling country of upper New York State. Life there was simple but it was not commonplace. It is well to be reminded that this region, now known for its rock-ribbed conservatism, once seethed and heaved with causes and passionately held convictions, with protests and bold idiosyncratic beginnings. In Troy, Emma Willard founded the Troy Female Seminary, in 1821, giving it a name at once precise, proud, and genteel. There girls were first offered a curriculum equal to that given boys — the necessary approach to preparing for a college education. At Fayette, Seneca County, Joseph Smith officially organized the Church of Jesus Christ of Latter-Day Saints, in 1830; Seneca Falls was host to the first convention to "consider the social, civil and religious conditions and rights of women," called by Lucretia Mott and Elizabeth Cady Stanton in 1848; and the Oneida Community, the best known of the several communistic societies, was established in 1847 by John H. Noyes. Like today's activists, men and women, singly and in groups, were challenging the foundations of education, the position of women, religion, and sex.

Canandaigua is fairly close to Seneca Falls and not distant from Troy. Ideas enunciated in those places spread far and were heard by willing ears. Lucretia Mott's personal declaration of independence, "I early resolved to claim for myself all that an impartial Creator had bestowed," could have been taken by Emily Smith for her own. Her father, Judge James Smith, supported her in her determination not to settle for the education deemed sufficient for a young lady of marriageable age from a well-to-do family — drawing, painting, light reading, English, perhaps French, with an M.R.S. as the only suitable degree. Instead she became a member of Bryn

Mawr's first graduating class, 1889, and a pioneer in seeking postgraduate study in England. She spent two years at Girton College, Cambridge, and on her return taught Greek at the Packer Collegiate Institute in the fashionable Heights section of Brooklyn. Two years' fruitful teaching and the publication of her translation from the Greek of sections of Lucian won her an invitation to join the classics department of the newly founded University of Chicago.

In 1894 — she was twenty-nine and already known for her scholarship — she became the first dean of the fledgling Barnard College. Certainly, the undergraduates, some fifty in all and each of them serious and earnest, had never met anyone quite like Dean Smith before. Years later one of them wrote that students "found her quick, sophisticated, humor often rather mystifying; she made it seem an amusing adventure to be getting an education against the will of the world." How were her students to know that it was her style to treat the struggle as an amusing adventure? She pinned the tail right on the donkey when, in her report to the trustees, she reaffirmed her belief that victory for the right for women to be educated would come "by the gradual conquest of experience over scruples, whether reasoned or prejudiced." Her equanimity encouraged the students to discard their militant stance: they

came to understand that they were not marching
on a crusade but rather that they had started on
the way to citizenship in the great world of ideas
and images, metaphors, and myths, wherein each
could choose the imperfect answers around
which to order her own life.

Dean Smith carried the work of both Emma
Willard and Lucretia Mott forward. Under her
guidance, Barnard College became part of Co-
lumbia University, thus bringing it into the
larger academic community; she related women's
struggle for an education to the larger social
struggle. From Lucretia Mott's experience, she
knew how easy it is for reformers to be parochial.
When the Motts, husband and wife, who together
had worked hard and risked much as active
abolitionists were sent as delegates to the International Anti-Slavery Convention in London,
Lucretia was barred from the hall because of her
sex. This was the impetus that started a new
cause: eight years later she had her own convention at Seneca Falls, to which men *were* invited.
Dean Smith saw also that, like sex, poverty was a
barrier to education. During her brief tenure, the
Alumnae Association started a student loan com-
mittee that offered loans on generous terms to
qualified girls unable to pay the $150 tuition fee.
This was the beginning of Barnard's involvement
with the larger community.

Dean Putnam — a new name with a disturbing sound. In 1899, Emily James Smith married George Haven Putnam, the distinguished publisher, a scholar and a fighter who had led the group that finally secured an international copyright which would protect the rights of another minority — writers. A few conservative trustees were alarmed. To them, Dean Smith's marriage could only mean that either Barnard would suffer from her divided allegiance or, worse still, that Mrs. Putnam would be distracted from her home duties. She was not surprised at the appearance of the nine-headed monster, what the Greeks called Hydra and the moderns Marriage-versus-a-Career, a monster that grows two heads for each one cut off. As it announced its presence then, so, still alive and with undiminished strength, it would be present at each graduation; even today it moans and carries on as women venture into new fields, whether as architects, enginneers, doctors, aviators, or jockeys, up and down the list of men's activities.

Neither Barnard nor the marriage suffered. But marriage, for the trustees, had been a high hurdle; the prospect of the dean as a mother was too much. No one considered that motherhood would have given a new dimension to the deanship of a woman's college; regretfully, they accepted Dean Putnam's resignation, in 1900. Although her position was gone, her tie to Barnard continued. Mrs. Putnam remained as a trustee before she returned as a teacher. It was then she again took up writing, an activity already begun with her translation of Lucian.

Her book *The Lady* was published in 1910. The book amplifies Emily James Putnam's striking remark made while she was still a dean: "We at Barnard are not greatly concerned in arguing what women can do, or even what is truly feminine. We are interested in opening every sort of opportunity to women; then we shall quickly discover what women can do, or even what is truly feminine."

Her book is an exploration of the manifold aspects and attitudes which are summed up in the term the "woman question." Today we are accustomed to learn about our own society by using anthropological data to compare the way different societies define the role of woman and how, within each definition, the women of that particular culture lived. Mrs. Putnam used history, our own history as we trace Western culture back to its Greek origins; she based her inquiry on contemporary writings that survive — not, as in anthropology, on the observations made by one person at one moment in time. If her material is not as exotic as that furnished by Samoa and New Guinea, it is quite as illuminating and, for all its familiarity, is as bizarre and unexpected. It may even have more relevance since there are fewer cultural variables to explain, discount, or juggle.

Why is Lucian mentioned? Because as the Greek writer she had selected to translate — denoting a long, intimate relationship — she clearly found his style attractive and his point of view congenial. The mention claims a kinship — however remote — for *The Lady* and thus places the book in a special category. Utilizing Northrop Frye's genealogical chart ("The literary ancestry of *Gulliver's Travels* and *Candide* runs through Rabelais and Erasmus to Lucian"), I would place Emily James Putnam with them. She too sets "ideas and generalizations and theories and dogmas over against the life they are supposed to explain." Like Gulliver in his travels, Mrs. Putnam in her tour through history breathes the same social concern and sustains a point of view with the same dry wit. Perhaps the difference separating genius from greatness is this: Swift and Voltaire, Rabelais and Erasmus, *created* societies so as to satirize the foibles in the mental attitudes they saw around them; whereas Mrs. Putnam *re-created* past societies so as to hold the mirror up to her contemporaries' "scruples, reasoned or prejudiced," as she had called their attitudes. A classic is a classic whether major or minor.

The book, then, though it appeared sixty years ago, is fresh. It is not dated, except for such trivia as the mention of "the American sleeping-car," a feature practically unknown to the present generation. What makes it so alive and lively is that Mrs. Putnam was not constrained by the sociological thinking of her day: the concept of progress as an article of faith. She did not corset her material to make it fit into the then fashionable mode. Instead she presented the ups and downs of the lady, that segment of the female sex which through contemporary records and pictures could be defined and evaluated. The lady is observed in eight periods, each offering a different social setting: "The Greek Lady," "The Roman Lady," "The Lady Abbess," "The Lady of the Castle," "The Lady of the Renaissance," "The Lady of the Salon," "The Lady of the Blue Stockings," "The Lady of the Slave States." Her story covers two and a half milleniums. Examining the woman question — the beliefs, attitudes, and expectations that mold the woman's behavior in each society — she also includes the house the lady lived in, the dress she wore, how she filled her leisure time: eight patterns from our past.

Yet *The Lady* is surprisingly pertinent. If the book begins far away and long ago in Athens, of the fifth century B.C., it is because it was then and there the lady's ambiguities were first stated and

from there that so many of our ideas have come,
including those on the woman question. In
Athens, Plato produced what Mrs. Putnam calls
"the boldest declaration of her independence
ever drawn," and she includes a summary of and
quotations from the *Republic;* and Aristophanes
parodied the lady's virtuous docility when he
created a Lysistrata who organized the women to
use coital power to force their men to end a sense-
less war. But their words went unheeded. Instead
it was Pericles whose famous oration enunciated
"in one short sentence" the ideal lady. "To a
woman not to show more weakness than is natural
to her sex is a great glory, and not to be talked
about for good or evil among men." After him,
Aristotle in a "quasiscientific" argument justified
the status quo, placing the woman along with the
slave and the child in subjection to adult free
men. "The slave has no deliberative faculty at
all; the woman has, but it is without authority,
and the child has it but it is immature." The
young, the slave, the woman — how contemporary is Aristotle's joining these three groups in
their subjection. We are witness to the way in
which the unrest of the students and the impatience of the blacks are related. Singly and together they are attacking attitudes that have denied them proper participation in their society.
And the lady?

Mrs. Putnam wisely stopped with the lady of the antebellum South, for she saw that boundaries no longer held the women of the leisure class apart and distinct. Today the class of the lady has been divided in many parts. We have High, Low, and Medium Society, Cafe Society and the Affluent Society; the Horse Set, the International Set, the Jet Set, and the Beautiful People, to mention a few. They merge one with another as their names and faces appear on the pages of glossy magazines and the women's sections of newspapers. Their movements and sources of income, their marriages and divorces, their homes, planes, yachts, their benefits, art collections, and sports are publicized so that they may be as recognizable as the stars of stage, screen, and TV. But if the lady is in many pieces which like Humpty-Dumpty cannot be put together again, the woman question remains. It is well to look at this, however briefly, and to note two subsequent events which should have affected the woman question: she was given the vote and the pill.

Suffrage, birth control, and the teachings of Freud and Marx — despite these, the woman question still remains unanswered. Looking for significant changes, one can say that her enfranchisement did not affect the woman question any more than universal male suffrage altered the class structure in England. Nor was she liberated by Freud, the fruits of whose psychological questing penetrated Western thinking. By phrasing her cultural ambiguities as the result of an ontogenetic penis envy, he called the frustrations women felt neuroses and prescribed analysis to cure them, a therapy to ease them into accepting their lot. Karen Horney, an early woman analyst, utilizing Freudian techniques dredged out of her patients' psyches a prevailing dread man felt for woman, a dread he customarily handled by disparaging her. Dr. Horney wrote: "The view that women are infantile and emotional creatures incapable of responsibility and independence in work is the work of the masculine tendency to lower their [women's] self-respect."

Nor have the revolutionary systems proposed by Marx-Lenin-Mao done much more than add the useful term "male chauvinism" to identify one part of the woman question. Whatever the systems claim or promise, it is the behavior of their followers that informs us: the dissidents who want to break with tradition by and large continue the traditional attitudes toward the women who are part of their movements. The language changes but the attitudes hold. Where personnel officers tell educated, professionally trained women applicants that "women have no place in big business or big jobs," the striking students call their female allies "chicks" useful only to do their typing. More indicative are the labels pinned on the considerable number of young women who join the widespread student protests: they are "freaks" or their political, professional, or sexual assertiveness is diagnosed as due to nymphomania. The equality ungrudgingly permitted them both inside and outside the student movement is that of being tear-gassed, clubbed, or jailed like the male students. In numerous confrontations, young women find that Lucretia Mott's sobering experience is being repeated: their sex denies them a role in policy making among those fighting for "participatory democracy."

Mrs. Putnam brought her annals to an end with the demise of the slave states because, however much she was involved in the woman question, she was a social historian, not a sociologist. From that vantage point she noted how each success raised new qualms, each vindication new objections. Seeded through her eight accounts and her introduction are insights that have meaning for today's women who hope to realize their potentials as wives and mothers and individuals in their own right — all three. Her views seem based less on a militant feminism and more on the theory that the greatest resource of a society is its people, and that to waste one-half of it is — as she might have said — silly. In terms of efficiency, it is a very high price our society pays to support the luxury of a woman question. Just as Mrs. Putnam was too tolerant to make harsh judgments on long-dead societies, so she was wise enough to know that there was no single answer to so complex a situation.

She might have pictured the woman question as struggling against Hydra, a mythic way of stating that there are situations and attitudes which do not yield easily to solutions and which, no matter how we think we have changed them for the better, persist. In her day myths were generally thought of as a literary form, stories about fabulous persons and events; the fantastic nature of the actions they related gave them their undying quality. Since first told by the Greeks, they have been part of Western culture.

More recently, however, myths have been studied as embodying widespread popular ideas about natural, cultural, or historical phenomena. Increasingly, social scientists, art historians, and literary critics have read myths both as *models of* cultural attitudes and behavior as well as *models for* such attitudes and behavior. Seen thus, myths have a twofold nature: on the one hand they reflect a society's beliefs and sanction its actions while, on the other hand, they are the forms by which beliefs and actions are molded. This new

concept of the myth's dual role can be seen in the
Oedipus myth: Freud interpreted it as expressing the model of an innate condition, whereas a
more recent view suggests that "we have got it
the wrong way round: that what happened was
that the myth of Oedipus informed and gave
structure to some psychological investigations at
this point." Or, consider the myths about Zeus's
numerous affairs with nymphs (pursued despite
Hera's vigilance and sulking and anger): the
myths may indicate that a patriarchal group of
conquerors imposed its principal god on tribes
each of whom theretofore had worshipped a goddess as their chief deity. Or such stories can also
sanction the double standard which permitted
sexual adventures to the male and denied them
to the female.

This new, more sophisticated handling of
myths might give a fresh approach to the woman
question which, in varying degrees and shapes, is
present in the societies Mrs. Putnam sketched.
Greek myths were part of their cultural tradition; they are a constant factor. All eight societies
were familiar with this mythology: names and
events are alluded to in the writings and are
iconographically present in the art of the different periods. The Greek myths were indestruct-
ible, persisting despite the advent of a new
religion, the formation of new economic and po-

litical systems, the discovery of a new world, and the profound changes created by new technologies.

Among the pertinent myths are those whose key words have entered our vocabulary, forming images and meanings even for those now unaware of their original context. Amazon, hubris, nemesis, Pandora — a Grecian quartet. The Amazons, so the myth tells us, were a tribe of women who assumed the role of men and won renown as fierce warriors. Their name itself means "without a breast," a name from which arose the mythic explanation that these masculine women amputated one breast to be able to shoot their arrows with greater accuracy. They were comely and their warlike nature did not keep them from seeking sex and bearing children — boy children were given away and the girls were reared as future Amazons. The fate of their queen, slain by the invincible Achilles while she fought on the Trojan side, was a warning to any Greek girl who might have wanted to be a tomboy and behave like a man.

Other myths carried other cautions. The Greek words *hubris* and *nemesis* have a feminine-gender ending, and this made it inevitable that they would enter mythology as female divinities. Hubris, whose birth is as dark as her purpose was evil, had only to touch men for them instantly to become mad; and Nemesis, a malign being, mercilessly carried out the dreadful fate imposed on all those touched by Hubris. One of the most popular myths tells of Circe, mistress of all enchantments, who enticed men to her palace with song, greeted them with smiles, entertained them with delicious food and drink, and, when they were drugged by her beauty and bounty, transformed them into swine. Pandora, too, is a familiar image. Hesiod, who tells all that we know about her, relates that she was sent as a messenger by the gods; clothed in a maiden's loveliness, she bore a box of gifts — all the pains and evils which would come to mankind.

We should not be surprised that the Greeks ascribed all maleficent happenings to women. The Judeo-Christian cosmology, the other source of our cultural heritage, affirms this with a loud amen: the sum of all the Greek female-centered myths equals Eve, the cause of man's downfall and expulsion from the Garden of Eden. Mrs. Putnam points out that "the decay of the aristocratic monastery was . . . a calamity for the lady, who was reduced to the old dilemma of the home or outlawry. Luther had a thoroughly Mohammedan notion of woman's status — only as a wife and mother had she a right to exist." The Protestant ethic took its values from the Bible, values sanctioned by the sacred myths of both the Old

and New Testaments. Not even veneration of the
Virgin Mary could wipe out the sin Eve let into
the world.

  With interest waning in Greek mythology and
in a belief in the literal interpretation of the Judeo-Christian cosmology, we are ready for new
myths which, in a time of rising secularization,
will be models for answers to the woman question. We need a woman with the caliber and style
of Emily James Putnam to look back on the old
myths and help create a mythology which, tran-
scending their cruel configurations, will truly
serve our times.

JEANNETTE MIRSKY

INTRODUCTION

The lady is proverbial for her skill in eluding definition, and it is far from the intention of the writer to profess to say what she is in essence. For the purpose of the present discussion she may be described merely as the female of the favoured social class. The sketches in this volume aim to suggest in outline the theories that various typical societies have entertained of the lady; to note the changing ideals that she has from time to time proposed to herself; to show in some measure what her daily life has been like, what sort of education she has had, what sort of man she has preferred to marry; in short, what manner of terms she has contrived to make with the very special conditions of her existence. Such an attempt, like every other inquiry into the history of European ideas, must begin with an examination of the Greeks. The lover of Greek literature knows it to be full of the portraits of strong and graceful women who were also great ladies. On the other hand the student of Greek history is aware that during the great period of the bloom of Athens the women

of the upper classes were in eclipse. **They were**
reduced to the condition commended **by** Lord
Byron in the passage made famous by Schopenhauer's approving citation: "Thought of the
state of women under the ancient Greeks—convenient enough. Present state, a remnant of
the barbarism of the chivalric and the feudal
ages—artificial and unnatural. They ought
to mind home—and be well fed and clothed—
but not mixed in society. Well educated too,
in religion—but to read neither poetry nor
politics—nothing but books of piety and cookery. Music—drawing—dancing—also a little
gardening and ploughing now and then. I have
seen them mending the roads in Epirus with
good success. Why not, as well as hay-making
and milking?"

The difference between the feminism of the
Greek in literature, art and social science, and
his anti-feminist practice cannot be explained
away, but a near view of some of its aspects
throws light both forward and backward upon
the history of the lady. At Rome she becomes
thoroughly intelligible to us. The society in
which she lived there is very similar in essen-
tials to that of our own day. We see the Roman
lady helping to evolve a manner of life so
familiar now that it is difficult to think it began
so relatively late in the history of Europe and

is not the way people have always lived. But if it is hard to realise the novelty in Roman times of a free, luxurious, mixed society in a great centre, it is even harder to picture its eclipse. The dark age put the lady back where Homer knew her; instead of a social creature she became again a lonely one, supported by the strong hand, kept safe from her enemies behind thick walls, and, as the price of safety, having but few friends. We have glimpses in Greek tradition of the lady in insurrection, refusing the restraint of the patriarchal family. In the dark age the insurgent Germanic lady makes her appearance, and by the oddest of paradoxes finds freedom in the cloister. The lady abbess is in some sort the descendant of the amazon.

The dying-out of violence and the consequent increase of comfort in private life, brought the lady once more into the stream of human intercourse. The movement called the Renaissance valued her as the most precious object of art, the chosen vessel of that visible beauty which men deemed divine. As conventional social life was organised in the sixteenth, the seventeenth and the eighteenth centuries, the lady's position became one of very great strength, reaching its climax in the career of the *salonière*. The great social changes that began to prevail at the end of the eighteenth century had a corresponding effect on the status of the lady and their work is not yet complete. In the United States during the two generations preceding the war for the union, the Slave States furnished the background for perhaps the last example the world will see on a large scale of the feudal lady. But the typical lady everywhere tends to the feudal habit of mind. In contemporary society she is an archaism, and can hardly understand herself unless she knows her own history.

Every discussion of the status of woman is complicated by the existence of the lady. She overshadows the rest of her sex. The gentleman has never been an analogous phenomenon, for even in countries and times where he has occupied the centre of the stage he has done so chiefly by virtue of his qualities as a man. A line of gentlemen always implies a man as its origin, and cannot indeed perpetuate itself for long without at least occasional lapses into manhood. Moreover the gentleman, in the worst sense of the term, is numerically negligible. The lady, on the other hand, has until lately very nearly covered the surface of womanhood. She even occurs in great numbers in societies where the gentleman is an exception; and in societies like the feudal where ladies and gentlemen are usually found in pairs, she soars so far above her mate in the development of the qualities they have in common that he sinks back relatively into the plane of ordinary humanity. She is immediately recognised by everyone when any social spectrum is analysed. She is an anomaly to which the western nations of this planet have grown accustomed but which would require a great deal of explanation before a Martian could understand her. Economically she is supported by the toil of others; but while this is equally true of other classes of society, the oddity in her case consists in the acquiescence of those most concerned. The lady herself feels no uneasiness in her equivocal situation, and the toilers who support her do so with enthusiasm. She is not a producer; in most communities productive labour is by consent unladylike. On the other hand she is the heaviest of consumers, and theorists have not been wanting to maintain that the more she spends the better off society is. In aristocratic societies she is required for dynastic reasons to produce offspring, but in democratic societies even this demand is often waived. Under the law she is a privileged character. If it is difficult to hang a gentleman-murderer, it is virtually impossible to hang a lady. Plays like The Doll's House and The Thief show how clearly the lady-forger or burglar should be differentiated from other criminals. Socially she is in general the product and the beneficiary of monogamy; under this system her prestige is created by the existence of great numbers of less happy competitors who present to her the same hopeless problem as the stoker on the liner presents to the saloon-passenger. If the traveller is imaginative, the stoker is a burden on his mind. But after all, how are saloon-passengers to exist if the stoker does not? Similarly the lady reasons about her sisters five decks below. There have been times when the primary social requirement has apparently been waived; it seems difficult, for instance, so to classify the lady as to exclude Aspasia and Louise de la Vallière. Nevertheless the true lady is in theory either a virgin or a lawful wife. Religion has given the lady perhaps her strongest hold. Historically it is the source of much of her prestige, and it has at times helped her to break her tabu and revert to womanhood. Her roots are nourished by its good soil and its bad. Enthusiasm, mysticism, renunciation, find her ready. On the other hand the anti-social forces of religion are embodied in her; she can renounce the world more easily than she can identify herself with it. A lady may become a nun in the strictest and poorest order without altering her view of life, without the moral convulsion, the destruction of false ideas, the birth of character that would be the preliminary steps toward

becoming an efficient stenographer. Senti-
mentally the lady has established herself as the
criterion of a community's civilisation. Very
dear to her is the observance that hedges her
about. In some subtle way it is so bound up
with her self-respect and with her respect for
the man who maintains it, that life would hardly
be sweet to her without it. When it is flatly put
to her that she cannot become a human being
and yet retain her privileges as a non-combatant,
she often enough decides for etiquette.

The product of many cross-impulses, exempt
apparently in many cases from the action of
economic law, of natural law and of the law of
the land, the lady is almost the only picturesque
survival in a social order which tends less and
less to tolerate the exceptional. Her history is
distinct from that of woman though sometimes
advancing by means of it, as a railway may help
itself from one point to another by leasing an
independent line. At all striking periods of
social development her status has its significance. In the age-long war between men and
women, she is a hostage in the enemy's camp.
Her fortunes do not rise and fall with those of
women but with those of men.

It seems pretty plain from the accounts given
us by the anthropologists of the ancient history
of our race that the gentleman appeared far

earlier than the lady.   Indeed the first division into social classes took place when the savage male captured a woman to work for him.   In view of the subsequent career of the lady, it is entertaining to note that she was for unnumbered ages submerged with all other women in the first menial and industrial class.   If to-day her husband toils that she may be idle, there was a time when the relation was reversed.   The first systematic leisure, we are told, was achieved by the man who discovered that the woman's occasional preoccupation with maternity gave him a chance to bring her into subjection. From that day he reserved himself for the tasks more congenial to his physique and his temperament,—pleasurable and exciting tasks, which soon became honourable since they were the badge of a privileged class.   These tasks were such as befitted the stronger, war and the chase, government and the chief offices of religion. To women was left all the work from which modern industrialism is derived, the patient, monotonous, undistinguished manipulation of nature that we call production.   Of course the chase was in its time productive too, when it was an essential contribution to the support of the group.   But with changed economic conditions its productive character faded out.   It remained

a gentlemanly occupation by virtue of its pleasurable aspect, but it has left no derivative in
modern industry. If anyone fancies that the
trade of the butcher represents the hunter's
occupation, he must remember that the butcher
of barbarism was the woman. Often the man
would not even bring the game to camp; when
it was slain his work was done, and the woman
came out to drag it home or to dismember it
where it lay.

The wise men who know about these things
seem inclined at present to allow us to think that
the first savage woman ranged free with her cubs,
killing for them and holding her own against
man and beast. She was no Artemis; her legs
were short, her arms were long, and her body was
hairy. But she had a sound social position.
Surviving in many places among the superim-
posed institutions of man-controlled society,
there are traces of the early system under which
the wife was not the husband's property, and
under which the maternal household was the
social unit. The child belonged to the mother
and took his name from her. Marriage was a
flexible arrangement, terminable at the woman's
will as well as at the man's. The permanent
thing was the tie between the mother and her
children which was the first social bond and

gave rise to curious forms of group organisation and to institutions that survived into historic times.

But by degrees the man took possession.
Perhaps the ownership of the husband in the
wife and the children known as the patriarchal
or proprietary family, was the result of a gradual
shift from more or less peaceful savagery to the
fighting-stage as involving wife-capture; and
wife-capture in its turn made the domestic subordination of even the women of the man's own
group seem right and fitting to all concerned.
Perhaps on the other hand the early woman was
undone simply by the inevitable working of the
maternal instinct. This led her to build a shelter for the child, to keep a fire, to experiment
with vegetable foods that she might not have to
leave her nest and range too far afield. The
early home of the mother and child became attractive to the man. It was a fixed point where
he knew he could find shelter and food. When
maternity had gone so far as to make woman
synonymous with both superior comfort and
inferior physique, the man moved in and made
himself master. At any rate by fair means or
foul two great human institutions were apparently inaugurated together, proprietary marriage and the division of society into masters and
servants.

By degrees the woman's enforced speciali-
sation of function by degrees affected her both
physically and psychologically. Her stature,
weight and muscular strength became ever more
noticeably less than those of the man, and to his
explosive mental action she opposed her illim-
itable patience. As the ground of gentility
came to lie more and more in superior prowess,
exerted gradually not only upon women but
upon the weaker men, it must have seemed to
the sociologists of early barbarism that woman
with her confessed and growing physical inferiority was debarred forever from the gentle
class. She had it is true certain moral holds
upon the veneration of the group, based chiefly
on her relation to the occult and her mysterious
connection with nature as the source of life. And
when the gentility of the strong man became
hereditary, his daughter had a theoretical share
in it. But these psychological claims to social
distinction for the woman were always checked
by the uncontrovertible fact of physical subjection. There was no thinkable way in which the
woman could emancipate herself; much less was
there a way in which she could conquer for
herself a foothold in the privileged class of men.
It must have seemed to her then that the only
escape from drudgery, which after all was
within her strength, lay through violence and

exploit which by this time were beyond it. Until changing economic conditions made the thing actually happen, struggling early society could hardly have guessed that woman's road to gentility would lie through doing nothing at all.

It would be interesting to note if we could the stages by which, through the accumulation of property and through the man's æsthetic development and his snobbish impulses acting in harmony, he came to feel that it was more desirable to have an idle than a working wife. The idle wife ranked with the ornamentally wrought weapon and with the splendid offering to the gods as a measure of the man's power to waste, and therefore his superiority over other men. Her idleness did not come all at once. One by one the more arduous tasks were dropped that made her less constant or less agreeable in unremitting personal attendance on her lord. The work that remained was generally such as could be performed within the house. Here we find her when history dawns, a complete lady, presiding over inferior wives and slaves, performing work herself, for the spirit of workmanship is ineradicable within her, but tending to produce by preference the useless for the sake of its social and economic significance. As is the case with any other object of art, her use-lessness is her use.

It follows from the lady's history that she is to-day, when freed from many of the old restrictions and possessed of a social and financial power undreamed of by her originators, a somewhat dangerous element of society. Her training and experience when not antisocial have been unsocial. Women in general have lived an individualistic life. As soon as the division of early labour sent the man out to fight and kept the woman in the house, the process began which taught men to act in concert while women still acted singly. The man's great adventure of warfare was undertaken shoulder to shoulder with his fellows, while the rumble of the tam-tam thrilled his nerves with the collective motive of the group. The woman's great adventure of maternity had to be faced in cold blood by each woman for herself. The man's exploit resulted in loot to be divided in some manner recognised as equitable, thus teaching him a further lesson in social life. The woman's exploit resulted in placing in her arms a little extension of her ego for which she was fiercely ready to defy every social law. Maternity is on the face of it an unsocial experience. The selfishness that a woman has learned to stifle or to dissemble where she alone is concerned, blooms freely and unashamed on behalf of her offspring. The world at large, which may have made some appeal to the sympathies of the disinterested woman, becomes to the mother chiefly a source of contagious disease and objectionable language. The man's fighting instinct can be readily utilised in the form of sports and games to develop in boys the sense of solidarity; the little girl's doll serves no such social end. The women of the working-classes have been saved by their work itself, which has finally carried them out of the house where it kept them so long. In the shop and the factory they have learned what the nursery can never teach. But the lady has had no social training whatever; the noticeable weakness of her play at bridge is the tendency to work for her own hand. Being surrounded by soft observance she has not so much as learned the art of temperate debate. With an excellent heart and the best intentions but with her inevitable limitations, the lady seems about to undertake the championship of a view of society to which her very existence is uncongenial.

As the gentleman decays, the lady survives as the strongest evidence of his former predominance. Where he set her, there she stays. One after another the fabrics that supported her have tottered, but she remains, adapting herself to each new set of circumstances as it arises. It is possible that an advancing social sentiment will extinguish her altogether, but she can never be forgotten.

THE LADY

THE LADY

THE GREEK LADY

"Phidias supported the statue of Aphrodite at Elis upon a tortoise to signify the protection necessary for maidens and the homekeeping silence that is becoming to married women."— PLUTARCH, *Concerning Isis and Osiris.*

I

UNDER the stress of sharp military competition the Greeks developed in the long run the conventional type of lady, who is distinguished from women at large by the number of things she may not do. It was necessary to the unstable equilibrium of a Greek state that she should be cut down to her lowest economic terms. She could not be dispensed with altogether for she was the necessary mechanism for producing legitimate heirs and could conveniently combine with this function the direction and management of her husband's house. To these activities and to her religious duties her life was restricted. She hardly appears in history. There is not a woman in politics in Athens from beginning to end. Herodotus' narrative is sprinkled with love stories when he treats of other states, but there is no trace of the sentimental motive in the dealings of Athens. The suppression of the woman of the upper class as an element of society is perhaps part of the price paid for the greatness of the city—the result of the working of social laws which probably could not at the time and under the conditions be resisted. The world has never yet seen a society that could afford to take care of all its members. The savage who kills his grandfather in the interests of the tribe starts with disgust from the missionary who lets fall that in Europe there are old gentlemen living in plenty while children starve. The inevitability of these sacrifices is proved by the general acquiescence of the victim. The old woman who is rescued by the missionaries escapes in the night and swims back to die as her clan morality requires. The poor in Europe have for centuries, sometimes with enthusiasm, acquiesced in the existence of the rich. And we have no record of attempted mutiny by the gentlewomen of Athens. The tabu separating them from the slave, the alien and the courtesan had its full mental effect, and they were made to cling to their doubtful privilege by the same psychic treatment as was used by Tom Sawyer to induce his playmates to whitewash the fence.

Ischomachos was a priggish young Athenian of good social position whom Xenophon has immortalised for us. When he married he made up his mind to educate his wife. She was a girl of fifteen, as brides often were in Athens, and, as he told Socrates, the greatest pains had been taken with her by her parents so that she might see as little as possible, hear as little as possible and ask the fewest possible questions. Ischomachos had a well-ordered mind. When the wife had been broken in and had grown used to her husband's hand (the phrases are his own), he laid down for her the proposition that they had pooled their goods and formed a partnership for two purposes: to produce children and to keep house. The question of the rearing of children he postponed until they should have some, but in regard to the house he defined very clearly their mutual relations. God and custom, he said, concurred in delimiting these.

Men are strong, therefore they must go out to contend with the elements and, if need be, with other men to get a living for their families. Women are physically weak, therefore God meant them to live in the house. They are timid while men are bold; they must therefore be stewards while men are acquirers. Women are naturally fonder of babies than men are; by this discrimination God beckons women to the nursery. Having apparently won his child-wife's consent to this familiar substitution of effect for cause, he explained her duties in detail. She was to organise the slaves, selecting some for out-door work, some for the house. She was to receive and store the supplies as they came in from the farm. Another department of her work was clothing the family. Every step from the reception of the raw wool to the turning out of the finished garment was to be taken under her eye. And there was one duty which the husband feared would be very disagreeable,—the care of any slave that might fall ill. But to this the little newly-tamed wife made a charming answer, an answer that casts forward many centuries to Elizabeth of Hungary and the frame of mind that we think of as "Christian." "That will be the pleasantest task of all," she said, "if it will make them fonder of me."

One day Ischomachos came in and asked for something which his wife, blushing for her incompetence, could not furnish him. He handsomely took the blame upon himself for not having set his goods in order before handing them over to her, and straightway gave her a lecture on the beauty of system. The army, the dance, the farm, the ship, all are adduced to prove the use and beauty of "a place for everything and everything in its place." Having completed his theoretical treatment of the subject, Ischomachos went over her new domain with his wife to start her right, and if we want to see just what her surroundings were we cannot do better than to follow his narrative.

"My house," he said to Socrates, "is a plain one, built with an eye to convenience alone. The character of each room determines its contents. Thus, our bedchamber is secure against thieves, therefore the best rugs and furniture are kept there. The dry part of the attic is the place for the food-stuffs, the cold part for wine, while the light rooms are the place for goods and work that need light. I pointed out to my wife that the beauty of the living-rooms lay in their exposure, which made them sunny in winter and shady in summer. Then I showed her the women's quarters, separated by a bolted door from those of the men. Next we proceeded to classify the gear. First we put together everything that had to do with the sacrifices. Then we grouped the maids' best clothes, the men's best clothes and their soldier outfits, the maids' bedding, the men's bedding, the maids' shoes and the men's shoes. We put

weapons in one group and classified under different heads the tools for wool-working, baking,
cooking, care of the bath and of the table and
so on. Then we made a cross-classification of
things used every day and things used on holi-
days only. Next we set aside from the stores
sufficient provision for a month, and also what
we calculated would last a year. That is the
only way to keep your supplies from running
out before you know it. After that we put
everything in its appropriate place, summoned
the servants, explained our system to them and
made each one responsible for the safety of each
article needed in his daily work and for restoration after use to its proper place. Articles used
only occasionally we put in charge of the house-
keeper with a written inventory. We showed
her where they were kept and instructed her to
give them out to the servants when necessary and
to see that they were all put back again.

"When all these arrangements were made,"
Ischomachos continued, "I told my wife that
good laws will not keep a state in order unless
they are enforced, and that she as the chief
executive officer under our constitution must
contrive by rewards and punishments that law
should prevail in our house. By way of apology
for laying upon her so many troublesome duties,
I bade her observe that we cannot reasonably

expect servants spontaneously to be careful of the master's goods, since they have no interest in being so; the owner is the one who must take trouble to preserve his property. To this my wife replied that it was as natural to a woman to look after her belongings as to look after her children, and that I should have given her a more difficult task if I had bidden her give no heed to these matters."

Socrates liked this. "By Hera," he cried, "your wife reasons like a man!"

Ischomachos was emboldened to further confidences. "One day I saw her with a lot of powder on her face to make her look whiter and a lot of rouge to make her look redder and high-heeled shoes to make her look taller. I pointed out to her in the first place that she was doing as dishonourable a thing in trying to deceive me about her looks as I should have done if I had tried to deceive her about my property. And then I remarked that though her arts might impose upon others, they could not upon me who saw her at all times. I was sure to catch her early in the morning before they had been applied, or tears would betray them, or perspiration, or the bath."

The little lady seems to have taken this also in good part, for she asked her husband how she should gain a genuine bloom if she must give up the semblance of it, and he gave her as sound advice as could be founded on the assumption that in the divine scheme whereby men and women complement each other, oxygen (as Professor Ward says) is for men and carbon dioxide for women. "I told her not to be forever sitting about like a slave girl but to stand at the loom, teaching what she knew and learning what she did not. I advised her to look on at the breadmaking and stand by while the housekeeper dealt out the supplies and go about inspecting everything. Thus she could practice her profession and take a walk at the same time. I added that excellent exercise could be had by making beds and kneading dough."

This passage from the *Œconomicus* is the most substantial document we have for the Athenian lady of the great period, but we can gather from scattered references a good deal of information, chiefly negative, to fill out the story of her life. She was received at birth with less enthusiasm than a boy-baby, for the question of her dowry began at once to weigh upon her parents. For aught we know, however, she had the same love and care and playthings as her brothers for the first few years of her life. But when the boys were handed over to the pedagogue and the schoolmaster, her way and theirs diverged forever. We do not know that she received any systematic education. Doubtless she could sometimes read and write; she learned from her mother a certain amount of household management and labour, and religious instruction was gilded for her by association with her only outings. When she was of marriageable age her parents picked out for her as desirable a young man as the dowry would fetch. She was betrothed with great ceremony, married with less, and lived as happily thereafter as her husband permitted. She was a perpetual minor in the eye of the law. Before marriage her father or nearest male relative was her guardian; after marriage, her husband. Her dowry passed into her husband's hands, subject to the provision that if he divorced her he must pay it back. Theorists considered carefully what the amount of the ideal dowry should be;—enough to secure the dignity of the wife's position, but not so much as to tie the husband's hands. She seldom left the house, never unattended by a female slave. At the religious festivals from which men were excluded she mingled freely with other women, but there was apparently little or no visiting from house to house. She was visible to the public only when from time to time she took part in a general religious ceremony or watched a pious procession. The peasant-women worked with their fellows in the fields, the market-women chattered in the agora, the courtesans came and went as they would and sharpened their wits by talk with all sorts of people. But the lady had no society but that of her slaves. She had social relations with no freeman save those of her family. If her husband dined alone at home she shared his meal, but if he had guests she was unseen. He lived mostly away from home in a man's world of a very high type. His life was carried on in the presence of magnificent objects of art and was stimulated by the exciting presence of great men. Naturally his home was not very amusing, and his wife seemed pretty nearly to be a creature of a different species. But he was scrupulous in his respect to her, very careful to use no unsuitable language in her presence and to maintain her good opinion of him. Romantic love is notoriously an invention of later times. Some aspects of it occur in Athenian life, but with different associations from those the words have for us. The tender, unselfish solicitude for the welfare of the beloved was felt sometimes by men for promising lads: the enthusiasm of passion was sometimes kindled by a gifted courtesan, educated by the conversation of the great men of her time. So serious a person as Demosthenes could say, as a platitude in a public address, "We have courtesans for pleasure, slave women for personal service and wives to bear us lawful offspring and be faithful guardians of our houses." "A wife," said Menander, "is a necessary evil." Anything that is necessary tends to become an evil, and the wife's dynastic importance, which was her very *raison d'être,* operated to her disadvantage as a source of romantic interest. What she thought of her lot we can only guess; tortoises leave no memoirs.

II

THE oddity of this lady's fate is striking. She lived in the house among a people that lived out of doors. So just-minded and scientific a man as Plato speaks of women as "a race that are used to living out of the sunlight." Among a people who gave great importance to physical training she was advised to take her exercise in bedmaking. At a period when the human spirit was at its freest she was enclosed on all sides. Art and thought and letters were reaching the highest development they were ever to know, but for her they hardly existed. All these contradictions, however, are intelligible in comparison with one that must immediately strike the reader. Any one who studies the literature or the art of the Greeks becomes aware of the existence at this period, as at every other in their history, of a deep seated, omnipresent feminism. If we can imagine Athens and its inhabitants revivified and inspected by a modern visitor, we can safely say that after a week's sojourn he would record in his note-book his strong impression of the reverent and admiring interest taken in women. High above the town and dominating every prospect stood the glorious temple and awful likeness of the hypostasis of womanhood who was the unifying spirit of the land. Beside the entrance to the citadel stood the shrine of the same great power in her lovely aspect of Victory. And in the adornment of both these temples the physical beauty of woman was enthusiastically rendered; young, vigorous and pure, those marble maids and matrons would cause our traveller's blood to thrill with envy of the land that held such women and thought of them so nobly. Wherever he went he would find the same powerful feminine motive in art, sometimes as the expression of a profound sentiment of the mystic character of woman and her relation to nature, sometimes the result of a sense of her sheer æsthetic value. She stands everywhere as man's equal, Hippodamia beside Pelops and Sterope beside Œnomaos. Sometimes she springs upon a horse and fights with man, nor is she always overborne. Sex has not made too great inroads upon her; she is not merely woman but a human being.

If our traveller was so fortunate as to be present at a theatrical representation, the impression he had received from plastic art would be reinforced. Ten to one the play would deal with the psychology or with the fate of some woman, who was also a great lady, the wife or the daughter of a king. She might be a devoted maiden, strong with the strength of mind and will that is generally ascribed to men only. The cause for which she lays down her life is not one of the popular causes supported by the emotion of the crowd which makes martyrdom easy; it is an idea reasoned out by herself alone. She goes to her death in the moral loneliness which is the heaviest of dooms. Or perhaps the heroine would be a gentle lady who dared to face the death her coward husband shrank from. Perhaps she would be a wild-eyed woman edging her brother's milder temper for a dreadful act of justice on their mother. She might be the proud victim of a hopeless love, betrayed by her false confidante; dying at last in shame and desperation she commits her first and only baseness, destroying the man she loves. Good or bad, she was always in the problem. If an exceptional play was now and then written without a woman in it, it but proved the rule, just as *Treasure Island* and *Dr. Jekyll* by their reactionary exclusion of the feminine interest prove its preponderance in modern fiction.

If it happened to be a comedy that our imaginary visitor witnessed, he might easily get another statement of the public interest in women. He might see a presentation of society under the equal suffrage, or a masterly application of the marital boycott to international affairs. Women of contemporary Athens would be credited with shrewd wits, political competence, the power of organisation and readiness in debate. He would note that it gratified the public to see the women outwit the men. If he was struck by the fact that there were no women in the audience, he would explain it readily enough by the extreme freedom of speech and action allowed on the stage.

If accident or foresight made our traveller's visit coincide with the celebration of the Greater Eleusinia, he would see the whole population occupied in the great religious act of the year. The ideas he had gained at school of the hierarchy of Olympus with Zeus at the head would crumble before the evidence of what was really vital in Athenian religious life—the cult of the

Mother, the giver of life, of her human sufferings, her divine power and her sacramental in-
stitutes. He had probably read in some text-
book of anthropology that the first use for
food of wild herbs and seeds and their subsequent culture are due to primitive woman.
The image of it in his mind would be some poor
Shoshone squaw with basket in one hand and
paddle in the other, beating out the seed of
the desert grass. But after he had for nine
days and nights participated with the Athenians
and the deputations from other states in their
great ritual, the image would have changed.
The squaw would be replaced by the figure of a
stately woman, both gentle and dread, a very
goddess, yet acquainted with grief. And with
the physical life given by her to men he would
learn to associate a spiritual life, begun on
earth and lasting forever, embodied in the
mysteries of her service;—mysteries of such a
nature that partakers in them, said Isocrates,
"have better hopes concerning death and all
eternity."

If our friend had the best introductions he
might conceivably be asked to dine with Pericles.
He would probably find a party of men only,
who were forming most of the ideas that the
race were ever to produce. These men by a
happy peculiarity would be as companionable

as they were learned. He would receive a strong impression of elevation of character without any kill-joy Puritanism. The gathering would be presided over by possibly the most charming woman the visitor had ever seen, a woman whose breeding and brains and beauty equipped her to practice the art of the *salonière* some two thousand years before Mme. de Rambouillet. And yet you could see, when now and then a glance passed between her and Pericles, that her chief interest lay in his career rather than in her own. "What is the name of Pericles' wife?" our ingenuous stranger might ask of a fellow-guest. "Ah, my dear fellow," the answer would be, "Aspasia is not exactly his wife. She was born in Miletus, you know, and an Athenian citizen is forbidden by law to marry an alien. So there they are. They have a child and live more correctly than many married people. She is all the wife he has and I should not advise any man to act on the hypothesis that she is anything else." The visitor would think he understood perfectly. "George Eliot," he would say to himself, turning back to the other guests. Very likely he would find them listening to a new theory of Socrates, which he was saying he had heard from the wisest person he knew, a woman, Diotima. The

company would smile, for Diotima was his
"Mrs. Harris."

Other hospitalities might be offered to our
lucky friend in the shape of meetings with men
at the gymnasia or other places of resort, where
the absence of women would not surprise him.
He might easily spend a delightful week in the
full stream of Athenian life, noting the pretty
women in the street, feeling everywhere the cult
of womanhood, and reflect only afterward that
by some odd coincidence he had not once been in
the same room with a woman of conventional
social position.

III

PERICLES is responsible for the classical
expression of what the men of his time
deemed "ladylike." In the famous oration attributed to him by Thucydides, he characterised in eloquent words the spirit of his
city, free, joyful and brave, the most inspiriting
place a man could wish to live in. "And if I
am to speak of womanly virtues, let me sum
them up in one short sentence: To a woman not
to show more weakness than is natural to her
sex is a great glory, and not to be talked about
for good or evil among men." We have seen,

however, that though in practice the Greeks had shorn the lady of all but negative qualities and left her hardly any room for unrestrained action, their art and their literature were nevertheless full of the tradition of a lady whose characteristic was freedom. Despite their singleness of mind, the Greeks like all mankind were capable of seeing the better and following the worse. Let us see how it happened that if all the ladies they saw were prisoners, nevertheless all the ladies they thought about were free.

Far in the background of civilised society, hardly to be recognised save by analogy with backward societies of our own day, there looms a shadowy vision of the state of things when women were in a very different relation to society from that which prevails to-day. The family in those times consisted of mother and child; and just as maternity is apparently no drawback in the long run to the fighting power of the lioness, we are at liberty to think that it did not necessarily result at once in the subjection of woman. Even after her physical subjection, she remained for a time the pillar of society. Her children were her property and through her they traced their descent. Her prestige was reflected in the cults of primitive men, for early gods were apt to be female and their rites to be conducted by women. This moment of equilibrium passed everywhere with the advance toward civilisation. Each step upward, the building of the hut, the kindling of the fire, the permanent attachment of the man to the mother and her child, was a step towards the social subordination of woman, a move made at her expense for the benefit of the child. Primitive conditions are generally brought to our knowledge with displeasing accessories. It is positive pain to many minds to think of a society that knew neither proprietary marriage nor the metals, and it was with many apologies that the anthropologists first suggested the widespread occurrence of the phenomenon. Before the fusion of races took place that produced the people whom we call Greeks, the lands they came to occupy were held by barbarous folk whose ways could not be altogether eliminated from the amalgam they formed with the invader. In a score of ways we can see how close barbarism was to the Greeks. They drew as it were a magic circle within which the monster could not come. But it prowled forever about the edge of light, howling and grimacing, until finally the spell failed and darkness prevailed again in Europe. Within the sacred ring the grewsome old facts were transformed, not consciously but by the genius of a people whose instinct was to see things in the best light. They knew there was some good reason, for instance, why by Attic law a man might marry his sister by the same father but not his sister by the same mother. They knew that their genealogical trees had a way of running back to a woman as the first ancestor. Herodotus in his day found Hellenic communities in which if you asked a man his family name he gave you his mother's. All these facts might have been as humiliating to the Greek of the patriarchal era as the Darwinian hypothesis was to the mid-Victorian. But the Greek stated them, naïvely, in terms that saved his self-respect as a member of man-controlled society. The primitive ancestress became a lovely princess, beloved of a god or married to a fair-haired invader from the north. Finding that women had once been of more social importance they endowed them instinctively with royal attributes. Great ladies like Jocasta and Helen and Clytemnestra they made of those dimly discerned traditional women with whose hand the title of a kingdom passed. But by far the most striking expression of their reminiscence of the old status of women, was the story of the Amazons. This tribe of warrior-women was ranged, it is true, with the powers of darkness. Between his adventures with the mares of Diomede and the oxen of Geryones,

Herakles had to subdue their queen, Hippolyta, and take her girdle from her; Bellerophon was despatched against them in Lycia, and they fought against the Greeks at Troy. But although the society they symbolised was part of the old order which the Greek could not suffer, he still felt the beauty that might come of a free, wild life for women not dominated and not oversexed. There is not a disrespectful word of the Amazons in Greek literature and the utmost resources of Greek art were used to render their lovely vigour and the sadness of its inevitable defeat. Too dangerous to be allowed among men, their type was perpetuated among the immortals in Artemis, the spirit of the wildwood, both boon and bane of all wild creatures, strong, fearless, unconquerable, with a strain of antique cruelty pointing plainly enough to her primitive origin. But Artemis, the bitter virgin, was denaturalised. The Amazons—and here precisely lay their menace to a man-governed world—shared the full human lot, mated with men worthy of them and bore children, a marvellous race since they sprang from warriors on both sides. But the male children were exiled from the state and the girls grew up to be like their mothers before them, crowning with chaste beauty the manly virtues of courage and honesty. Though the evolution of Greek society proceeded to the complete social subjection of women it never lost sight of the glory of the alternative course. We may almost say that the social situation was symbolised in the tradition of Achilles' regret when he had slain Penthesilea in combat before Troy. As he looked upon her lying dead at his feet he grieved that he had overcome her and thought how much better it would have been had he taken her to wife.

Thus did the Greeks picture to themselves a group of knightly ladies to represent the obstinate and irreducible element in primitive maternal society. The compromises by which the more ductile communities shifted toward the predominance of the male are also shadowed forth in the world we know as Homeric society. Everyone knows how Odysseus, shipwrecked, naked and starving, slept the sleep of exhaustion in the wood by the sea in the land of the Phæacians and how he was roused by the cries of the princess Nausikaa and her maidens playing at ball. When the hero emerged among them, a haggard, wild-eyed tramp, the handmaidens, already of the school of thought that deems your true lady a timid thing, fled screaming in panic. But the princess, exemplar of a better breeding, stood her ground and heard what the suppliant had to say. Brave, cool and of independent judgment, the girl considered all the circumstances of the case, weighing the stranger's good address against his alarming appearance and his evident need of instant succour against possible infraction of the *convenances*. Her good management of the situation, her charming girlish dignity and the liberty she took of falling in love with the man she had saved, prepare us for finding that she lived in a land where women had very lately been in a strong social position. The text says that Nausikaa's mother Arete was married to Alkinoos, her own father's brother, a consanguinity that did not count where descent was traced through the female line. "And Alkinoos took her to wife, and honoured her as no other woman in the world is honoured, of all that nowadays keep house under the hand of their lords. Thus she hath, and hath ever had, all worship heartily from her dear children and from her lord Alkinoos and from all the folk who look on her as on a goddess and greet her with reverent speech when she goes about the town. Yea, for she too hath no lack of understanding. To whomso she shows favour, even if they be men, she ends their feuds."* This is an invaluable expression of the Greek notion of a lady of the

* "Odyssey," trans. by Butcher and Lang.

old régime, sitting as judge among her people and honoured like a god. But it will be noted that the lady now has a lord, and that man-made propriety controls the free spirit of Nausikaa.

In spite of the traces of an older order, Homeric society in general shows woman subordinated, and in consequence a great efflorescence of the lady. The man is the head of the family and requires strict fidelity from his wife. He, however, is permitted the patriarchal privilege of minor wives who are generally bondswomen. The lady thus assumes her well-known social status; her faithfulness is the condition of her welfare, and she is indemnified for the discomfort of having rivals by the added lustre which their inferior condition confers upon hers. The Homeric lady is bought of her father by her bridegroom, and it is honourable to her when the price is high. "She who brings cattle" is the epithet of an attractive girl. Her marriage is arranged by her father, without regard to sentiment. The eternal question as to the relative chance of happiness in the marriage of *convenance* and that of inclination may be illumined by Homer's evidence. Andromache, Hector's wife, was *polydoros* ("bought with many gifts"), she passed as a chattel from her father to her husband; but the world has yet to imagine a more touching relation between man and wife than that of Andromache and Hector. The whole story of the lot of woman-kind under feudal institutions is told in the famous passage of the last parting of these two. -Hector going out to fight sought his wife to bid her farewell. She clasped his hand and weeping prayed him to remember what war means to women. "Dear my lord, this thy hardihood will undo thee, neither hast thou any pity for thine infant boy, nor for me forlorn that soon shall be thy widow; for soon will the Achaians all set upon thee and slay thee. But it were better for me to go down to the grave if I lose thee; for never more will any comfort be mine, when once thou, even thou, hast met thy fate, but only sorrows. . . . Nay, Hector, thou art to me father and lady mother, yea and brother, even as thou art my goodly husband. Come now, have pity and abide here upon the tower, lest thou make thy child an orphan and thy wife a widow." *

But great Hector of the glancing helm loved honour more, and answered her: "Surely I take thought for all these things, my wife; but I have very sore shame of the Trojans and Trojan

* "Iliad," trans. by Lang, Leaf and Myers.

dames with trailing robes, if like a coward I shrink away from battle." *

'The life of the Homeric lady was busy and free. She wrought at pleasant household tasks among her maidens, weaving the stuffs needed for everyday use and performing also those wonders of artistic needlework that always play so large a part in the life of the lady. She lived in a palace built strongly to withstand attack, such a palace as still exhibits its ground-plan amid the ruins of Tiryns. When a stranger had been allowed to pass the great gates he would have found himself in a large court-yard, open to the sky but surrounded by a covered colonnade. This court-yard would not impress a modern visitor as a satisfactory entrance to a great lord's house. Here the animals stood that were to furnish the day's dinner and here they were slaughtered. Here beggars were allowed to sit, and here was transacted a great part of the household business that we relegate to unseen regions. From the court a stately portico led to the great hall, the heart of the house, where on the central hearth, between the four pillars that sustained the roof, the fire was kindled. Beside the hearth stood two great chairs, one for the lord and one for the lady. These chairs were of

* The same.

cedar and ivory, inlaid with gold and silver, and there were many other chairs and small tables, all rich in material and workmanship. The ill-lighted room was brightened by covering the doors and walls with metal plates, often of bronze but sometimes of silver and gold. Sheets of blue glass were used for the same purpose, and sometimes painted pictures. Gleaming armour was also ranged along the walls, but this and the other metal-work suffered from smoke, which in the absence of a chimney escaped as best it might through an opening in the roof above the fireplace. The floor was of hard lime-cement mixed with pebbles. In this hall the meals were eaten and the whole of social life went on. Here after supper the minstrel took his harp and sang the deeds of heroes. At night the family was widely distributed. The lord and lady had their own chamber; the daughters and maid-servants slept in a quarter apart, sometimes on an upper floor. The sons of the house had each a room to himself built in the court, and visitors had beds laid for them in the portico. In a bathroom flagged with limestone stood the polished bath, which was in frequent requisition. The small objects in daily use, the earthen pots and jars, the curiously wrought weapons, testify to the sense of beauty and the refinement of life that surrounded the Homeric lady. A special part of the house was set apart for her and her women, but she came and went freely, though apparently never unattended. Her easy, sheltered life and personal elegance are reflected in the frequent reference to her white arms, her trailing dress, her fragrant bosom. Her ordinary garment was the *peplos,* a great woollen web, capable of much variety in the draping. It was held in place by a girdle, richly embroidered and clasped with gold. She wore also by way of ornament a necklace, a frontlet and earrings of gold. On ceremonious occasions she wore a veil, of finer tissue than her *peplos.* Generally her garments were "shining white," but sometimes they were coloured and the commonest colour was purple; they were washed in the streams, as clothes are still commonly washed in Greece, and dried on the rocks and the grass. Her personal belongings were rich and curious, and handmaidens waited on her at every step. When Telemachos visited Menelaos, his hostess made her appearance like a very fine lady indeed: "Helen came forth from her fragrant vaulted chamber, like Artemis of the golden arrows; and with her came Adraste and set for her the well-wrought chair, and Alcippe bare a rug of soft wool, and Phylo bare a silver basket which Alcandre gave her, the wife of Polybus, who dwelt in Thebes of Egypt. His wife bestowed on Helen lovely gifts; a golden distaff did she give, and a silver basket with wheels beneath, and the rims thereof were finished with gold. This it was that the handmaid Phylo bare and set beside her, filled with dressed yarn, and across it was laid a distaff charged with wool of violet blue. So Helen sat her down in the chair and beneath was a footstool for the feet." *

Although the presence of the minor wife is abundantly visible in the background of Homeric society, the tendency is nevertheless in the direction of monogamy. In the families that are, so to speak, in focus there is but one wife as there is but one husband. Sincere and robust affection between man and wife and the passionate love of both for the children is the norm. If the picture seems too rosy to be true, we must remember that Homer's goldsmith's work also seemed to be beyond the probable until it began to be recovered out of the earth. Now that we have been driven to believe him about dagger-blades, we may perhaps trust him further in the matter of married love. There was every reason why the lady should cling to her lord, for his strong arm only held her on her height. Any woman

* "Odyssey," trans. by Butcher and Lang.

whose protector failed her might become a
slave. Moreover she was her lord's property,
and in case of misdemeanour on her part he held
the patriarchal power of life and death. In
her husband's absence her own son was her
master. Penelope was bullied by Telemachos
and was proud of his manly self-assertion. But
she in her turn was absolute mistress of her
slaves, and had no reason to be dissatisfied with
her position in a system that placed so many
below her and so few above her.

When we speak of Homeric society we assume that the Homeric poems deal with an
actual state of things and with a single period.
These assumptions are doubtless both false, and
no department of scholarly research is more
attractive than that which is devoted to under-
mining them. It is nevertheless legitimate for
our purpose to view them naïvely as the record
of a wonderful world, wherein men used an
amazing language that never was spoken by
living man, and saw sights and did deeds that
were never part of human experience. We may
legitimately look upon them thus, for doubtless the historic Greeks of the great period
themselves did so, and far more important than
the scientific character of the poems is the effect
they had on the collective mind of the race that
evolved them. It must be constantly borne in

mind, in estimating the Greek's ideal of a lady, that there never was a time when he would not have admitted theoretically that she should be of the heroic type. Literature never ceased to take its women from the early legends, philosophers and satirists were always attracted by the hypothesis of social equality between the sexes, and at the time when militarism and democracy had done their worst for the lady, she might easily in her infrequent walks abroad come upon a sculptor modelling a magnificent young creature on horseback who, in spite of what he saw about him, persisted as his idea of woman.

IV

ONE of the temperamental differences between Plato and Aristotle consists in the greater willingness of Aristotle to acquiesce in existing conditions and to exert his imagination to provide reasons for their permanence. Plato's imagination urged him to view existing conditions in a different and more critical light. Nowhere does the difference come out more strong'v than in their views of the woman-question. There was room for a comparative study of it, based not only on traditions of the past but on the actual case at

Sparta, where women enjoyed greater social freedom than at Athens, shared the physical training of the men and held property. Aristotle, however, noted that in the society with which he was most familiar, the woman, the slave and the child were in subjection to men. Assuming that this is the best of all possible arrangements, he gives it a quasi-scientific basis: "The slave has no deliberative faculty at all; the woman has, but it is without authority, and the child has it, but it is immature." He notes that the occupations of women are different from those of men and shows that this must be so: if the women go into the fields with the men, who will manage the house? "It is absurd to argue from the analogy of animals that men and women should follow the same pursuits; for animals have not to manage a household." It will be seen that the mind of Aristotle does not in this connection rise far above that of Ischomachos. They agree that God and custom have placed women indoors.

Plato, on the other hand, realised that as women had not always lived in the shadow they might conceivably emerge again into the sunlight. He was possessed by the thoroughly scientific idea of the solidarity of the race. Could it be permanently good for the state that half of its adult free population should lag behind the other half in body and mind? He saw that a negative answer would carry him very far, but perhaps the farther the better. In the course of organising an ideal state in which the upper class, not primarily pursuing its own happiness, should be the disinterested guardian of the whole, he described as an essential part of that class such a lady as the world had never seen. There was to be no assumption that she had or lacked this or that faculty; custom had made certain distinctions but whether God concurred in them was to be determined by experiment. The girls of this chosen class were to be educated in every respect like the boys; Amazons were once more to be seen, but this time not opposed to men. Peaceful sports and warlike exercise were to develop the physique of boys and girls alike, and the training of the mind was to be the same for both. We are still uncertain whether there are actually psychic "sex-characters" or not; Plato could not see evidence of any. The different parts played by men and women in the continuance of the race seemed to him to have no necessary connection with their relative ability to practice medicine or to play the flute. We grant, he urged, that a bald-headed man is very different in one regard from a long-haired man; shall we then say that if bald men may become cobblers, long-haired men may not? And similarly, if we are sending for a doctor, shall we try to get one who excels in professional skill, or one who performs this or that function in reproduction? "None of the occupations which comprehend the ordering of a state belong to woman as woman, nor yet to man as man, but natural gifts are to be found here and there in both sexes alike; and, so far as her nature is concerned, the woman is admissible to all pursuits as well as the man. Shall we then appropriate all duties to men and none to women? On the contrary, we shall hold that one woman may have talents for medicine and another be without them; and that one may be musical and another unmusical; one woman may have qualifications for gymnastic exercises and for war, and another be unwarlike and without taste for gymnastics; there may be a love of knowledge in one woman and a distaste for it in another. There are also some women who are fit and others who are unfit for the office of guardian. As far as the guardianship of the state is concerned, there is no difference between the natures of the man and of the woman, but only various degrees of weakness and strength. Thus we shall have to select duly qualified women also, to share in the life and official labours of the duly qualified men, since we find that they are competent to the work, and of kindred nature with the men."*

It is well known that to secure the best public service from his governing class, both men and women, Plato made a clean sweep of property and the family from among them. Temporary unions were to be arranged by the state, children were to be reared by the state, dwellings and mess-tables were to be furnished by the state. These proposals met the same objections then that they meet now. Whether property and the status of women are indissolubly connected is still the fundamental social question. The thing to be noted by students of the lady is this new conception of her. Like the lady of feudalism, she is the female of a governing class, yet she is not economically dependent. Like the Christian nun, she is explicitly devoted, not to the pursuit of happiness, but to the service of others; yet she is not to forswear marriage and maternity. We must add to the historic oddity of the discrepancy between the actual Athenian lady and the lady of art, her still more striking contrast with this theoretical lady. A time of her deep subjection produced the boldest declaration of her independence ever drawn. Other men had thoughts

---

* Condensed from the "Republic," Book v., trans. by Davies and Vaughan.

on this subject similar to Plato's. The comedies of Aristophanes show a thorough understanding of the problem and prove that the general public must have been familiar with it. It could not logically fail to interest men who lived beneath the shadow of Athena, of that spirit of self-restraint who caught Achilles by his yellow hair to hold him back from murder, that spirit of wisdom who walked with Odysseus as his familiar friend, and whom in all her aspects they held to be typically feminine. There was no incongruity in broaching in her presence a bold view of the destiny of women. The really humorous paradox is that Pericles, standing up to voice the ideals of the people she had formed, should take no further account of the sex she was one of than to beg its representatives on earth to be at all costs ladylike.

THE ROMAN LADY

I

"All men rule over women, we Romans rule over all men, and our wives rule over us."—CATO THE CENSOR.

THE Romans, who were notoriously willing to consider their genius for conquest as compensation for some sorts of genius that were denied them, were nevertheless unable completely to conquer their women. With the best will in the world they never succeeded in simplifying the problem as the Greeks had done. Though the Roman lady was theoretically in the same position as the Greek lady, she was in practice a different species. Ordinary usage speaks of "the women of Greece and Rome" as if they were interchangeable. In this regard as in too many others, it is popular to dwell on certain formal points of likeness between the two great rival races rather than on essential points of difference. Greece and Rome have in fact suffered the fate that, according to Madame Cardinal, has overtaken Voltaire and Rousseau: *"Il paraît que, de leur vivant, ils ne pouvaient pas se*

39

sentir, qu'ils ont passé leur existence à se dire des sottises. Ce n'est que depuis leur mort que les deux font la paire." In regard to the present question, the formal likeness which they have in common with other patriarchal societies is that both held women to be perpetual minors. In Rome as in Athens, a woman was subject to her father or his representative until she became subject to her husband. But while at Athens the spirit of the law prevailed and harmonised with the general social sentiment, in Rome it was in opposition to social sentiment and was gradually modified by legal fictions and other compromises until it bloomed into one of those complete anomalies that make us feel how similar ancient society was to our own. This feeling is much more frequently evoked by the history of Rome than by that of Greece. The Greek is after all too exceptional and too uncompromising to be quite companionable. But with the Roman there come into history many of the limitations, the cross-purposes, the makeshift substitutes for high intelligence, the feeling, for instance, that it is more gentlemanly to be able to buy pictures than to be able to paint them, the Philistinism, in a word, that makes the world seem homelike.

Apart from the tendency to blend her with the Greek lady, another historical fallacy has been at work to obscure the features of the lady of Rome. She has suffered more than most from representation by types. In thinking of her one recalls chiefly extreme cases. The imagination flits bewildered from Lucretia to Messalina, from Cornelia mother of the Gracchi to Agrippina mother of Nero. Tradition and the partisan have done their best to fix upon her a rather inhuman character, whether for virtue or for vice. It is a study of some interest to try to discover the human meaning of her various presentations and to form a picture of her out of more reconcilable elements than mere antithesis.

Although the documents for early Greek history carry us much farther back in time than those for Roman history, the rising curtain nevertheless reveals the Roman in an earlier social stage than the Greek, for he is apparently still marrying by capture. While women have to be stolen by a community, their numbers will be relatively small; there will probably not be enough to go around. Among the Romans the natural results seem to have comprised a certain social importance for women and a strict monogamy for men as well as for women. Under these conditions it was apparently not necessary to seclude a wife; at any rate the Roman matron of all periods enjoyed personal freedom,

entertained her husband's guests, had a voice
in his affairs, managed his house, and came and
went as she pleased. In early days she shared
the labours and the dangers of the insecure life
of a weak people among hostile neighbours.
It may not be fanciful to say that the liberty
of the Roman woman of classical times was the
inherited reward of the prowess of her pioneer
ancestress, in the same way as the social freedom
of the American woman to-day comes to her
from the brave colonial housemother, able to
work and, when need was, to fight. It would
have been as difficult to find the lady in early
Italy as in early Massachusetts. There were
no courtesans for her to be distinguished from,
and there were relatively but few slaves; nor
was there so much wealth as to fix a gulf between rich and poor. There is nothing in
Roman traditions that corresponds in the least
with Homer's lady. The lady came fast enough
upon the Roman with all his other troubles,
but before that time the strong woman of the
plain old days had become a fixed tradition, endowed with heroic attributes and invoked to
shame the singular product of wealth and cos-
mopolitanism that took her place. The historic Roman idealised the virtues of early
history as shown by his ancestors, precisely as
he idealised them when he encountered them

again among the Germans. The reverence for women, their chastity and their physical courage, seemed in each case a wonderful deviation from human nature as he knew it. The conditions that produced the lady, as well as most of the other complexities of his life, were in general the result of his contact with alien civilisations.

One creative act however which he accomplished independently helped to produce the lady; the early organisation, namely, of Roman society on an aristocratic basis. As the group of tribal elders hardened into the Roman senate, it gave rise to the patrician class with the characteristic of hereditary privilege. Thus the Roman introduced pride of birth as a social motive. While he was still poor and illiterate he became "noble," and his wife became, in the most artificial sense possible, a lady. We see her of course through the softening medium of literary treatment; her industry, her physical courage, her self-devotion to the family and the clan, her appreciation of honour from the man's point of view, were traits that grouped themselves harmoniously about the great names of Hersilia and Lucretia and Valeria and Volumnia. Shakespeare's vision of her is hardly more enthusiastic than Plutarch's, from which indeed it was derived. Plutarch roundly declared that he could not subscribe to Thucydides's famous definition of the virtue of women—that it should consist in their being spoken of as little as possible, whether for praise or blame. "The Roman practice is best," he said, "by which the funeral eulogy is publicly pronounced over a dead woman as freely as over a dead man." And his pages are full of references to the excellences of the dead women of old. This early Roman lady, shining with tribal virtues, survived only sporadically in history. We may almost say that Cornelia supports unaided the weight of the majestic tradition. The fragments of her letters to her surviving son after the murder of his brother, may easily be genuine, and they bear out the view of her character taken by posterity. Unquestionably Cornelia proves something for the existence of the old type, but it must not be forgotten that she would be an exceptional person in any age. Single episodes are reported in which other ladies behaved as the theoretical *domina* should; Porcia and Arria hand on the torch. But they excite among their contemporaries the wonder always roused by an anachronism. Just as the western world stood aghast at the prodigies of Japanese warfare, in which the most modern science was used as the weapon of a tribal psychology long outgrown elsewhere, so the Rome of Claudius's time marvelled at Arria's smoking dagger. In general it must be confessed that when the Roman lady comes upon the historic stage she has already developed some of the characteristics that were to make her a perplexing element of society. Her force of character and the freedom to which she had been accustomed were certain to play havoc with the patriarchal system as soon as circumstances should give opportunity, and opportunity was given almost as soon as history begins.

From the beginning of Roman expansion in the third century before Christ, the Roman husband was frequently and for long periods away from home. The wars with Carthage, the wars in the East and in Spain, the wars in northern Europe, drew the patrician abroad as systematically as the Crusades drew the knights of later Europe. In each case profound changes resulted in the character, or at any rate in the demeanour of the lady. The first breaking down of her old social status seems to have been in the direction of allowing her to hold property. The marriage ceremony which passed her as a ward from the hand of her father to that of her husband was so modified as to leave a married woman theoretically subject to the *patria potestas,* and therefore to prevent her property from passing to her hus-

band. The effect of this arrangement appears
on the whole to have been her financial independence. She could evidently receive legacies,
for special legislation was needed at the end of
the Punic wars to prevent women of the
wealthiest class from doing so. The feeling of
patriarchal society is always strongly against
the economic independence of women. Aristotle believed its prevalence in Sparta to be one
of the causes of decadence. The ancient lady
could in no wise create property for herself,
and the men who had acquired it by labour or
conquest felt the unfairness of allowing it to be
controlled by a parasite. Just after the close
of the Punic war, in which Rome's economic
sufferings were very great, the Roman ladies re-
belled against certain sumptuary legislation
which specifically curtailed their expenditure.
The famous speech of Cato, opposing the repeal
of the Oppian law, is, as reported by Livy, an
expression of the ever-recurrent uneasiness of the
male in the presence of the insurgent female,
and in particular of the dislike of women which
we shall find a pretty constant factor in the
Roman's temperament.

"If, Romans," said he "every individual
among us had made it a rule to maintain the
prerogative and authority of a husband with
respect to his own wife, we should have less

trouble with the whole sex. It was not without painful emotions of shame that I just now made my way into the forum through a crowd of women. Had I not been restrained by respect for the modesty and dignity of some individuals among them I should have said to them, 'What sort of practice is this, of running out into public, besetting the streets and addressing other women's husbands? Could not each have made the same request to her husband at home? Are your blandishments more seductive in public than in private, and with other women's husbands than your own?'

"Our ancestors thought it not proper that women should transact any, even private business, without a director. We, it seems, suffer them now to interfere in the management of state affairs. Will you give the reins to their untractable nature and their uncontrolled passions? This is the smallest of the injunctions laid on them by usage or the laws, all of which women bear with impatience; they long for liberty, or rather for licence. What will they not attempt if they win this victory? The moment they have arrived at an equality with you, they will become your superiors." *

The love of excitement which was a temper-

* Livy, trans. by D. Spillan, Cyrus Edmonds, and W. A. M'Devitte.

amental trait of the Roman lady of history became a dangerous matter. It was natural that strong-willed women, exceedingly like the men of their race in body and mind, should seek for some equivalent of the adventures their husbands were engaged in the world over. They had not been tamed as had the ladies of Athens by the slow action of long ages of masculine encroachment. They were much nearer the soil and freedom. The men had not had time to bring them thoroughly into subjection, and yet were both unable and unwilling to set them free. Both sexes were in a false position, and overt acts of warfare became common. Livy reports three cases of husband-murder in noble families in thirty years. Divorce became a general practice. Not only the frivolous used it but the staid. Men had to be persuaded into matrimony as a duty. The excellent Metellus Macedonicus started a propaganda of marriage on patriotic grounds, and his pessimistic argument became a classic: "If we could get along without wives," he is reported to have said, "we should all dispense with the nuisance. But since nature has decreed that we can neither live very comfortably with them nor at all without them, we should consult rather our permanent good than our temporary happiness."

All these things were table-talk while Cornelia was still living. All about her was a welter of feminine discontent. Gradual amelioration of the marriage law was accompanied by an invention whereby even an unmarried woman might hold property and control it; she could contract a fictitious marriage, dissolve it at once, choose a guardian to suit herself and through him as a dummy administer her own estate. These changes, however, while enlarging the lady's power gave her nothing to satisfy her ambition and keep her out of mischief. Ethically her situation was a dangerous one, and many elements of safety were withdrawn when wealth, culture, exciting new religions, diseases, slaves and philosophy were brought to Rome as spoils of war.

II

THE unfortunate reaction upon the Romans of their achievements is a commonplace of history. The best of them were reduced in numbers by centuries of constant warfare, and the survivors were assailed by those bacilli of civilisation which always ravage a fresh race with a virulence unknown among the peoples that have become adapted to them. And the conditions that proved in the long run fatal to the noble Roman worked rapidly and perniciously upon his wife. With the introduction of slavery, what occupation the lady had was gone. She resigned the care of her house, the care of her children, the care of her person to Greek slaves who understood all these matters a great deal better than she did. The time that was left on her hands she filled with the pseudo-activities of the *nouveau riche*. Through her efforts "society" was organised for the first time in Europe. What people wore, what they ate and drank, what sort of furniture they had and how much their horses cost were questions that then for the first time acquired the importance they have ever since retained. The Greeks who, to be sure, had nothing in their dwellings that was not beautiful, had still supposed that great works of art were for public places. With the Romans began the private collection of *chefs-d'œuvre* in its most snobbish aspect. The parts played by the sexes in this enterprise sometimes showed the same division of labour that prevails very largely in a certain great nation of our own day that shall be nameless: the husband paid for the best art that money could buy, and the wife learned to talk about it and to entertain the artist. It is true that the Roman lady began also to improve her mind. She studied Greek and hired Greek masters to teach her history and philosophy. Ladies flocked to hear lectures on all sorts of subjects, originating the odd connection between scholarship and fashion which still persists. Their annexation of the field of letters was exceedingly annoying to their husbands. "I hate the woman," says Juvenal, "who is always turning back to the grammatical rules of Palæmon and consulting them; the feminine antiquary who recalls verses unknown to me, and corrects the words of an unpolished friend which even a man would not observe. Let a husband be allowed to make a solecism in peace." A husband naturally preferred in woman the kind of culture attained by the amiable Calpurnia, Pliny's wife. He says of her that she delighted to read and read again her husband's works, having no other schoolmaster than love. Like Rousseau's Sophie, the Roman lady should have had *du goût sans étude, des talents sans art, du jugement sans connaissance.*

A woman of fashion, we are told, reckoned it among her ornaments if it were said of her that she was well-read and a thinker, and that she wrote lyrics almost worthy of Sappho. She too must have her hired escort of teachers, and listen to them now and then, at table or while she was having her hair dressed,—at other times

she was too busy. And often while the philosopher was discussing high ethical themes her
maid would come in with a love-letter and the
argument must wait till it was answered.
Thesmopolis, a stoic philosopher, told his friend
Lucian of a mortifying experience. He was
attached to the suite of a great lady who took it
into her head to make a journey and invited
Thesmopolis to go with her. He found in the
first place that his companion in the carriage
was an effeminate youth, a pet of his mistress,
who had the painted face, the womanish head-
dress and the rolling eye of his class. Thesmopolis was an elderly man with a long white
beard, respectable to the last degree. He suffered extremely from his companion who sang
and whistled on the road and would have stood
up and danced in the carriage if he had not been
forcibly restrained. But presently this annoyance was overshadowed for the lady halted
her own carriage and called to her philosopher.
"Will you do me a favour?" said she. "Anything in my power," said he. "You dear, kind
man," said the lady, "take my lap-dog. She
is not well and I cannot make the servants pay
any attention to her. Indeed they don't even
take care of me. But I can trust her to your
tender heart." Thesmopolis could not refuse.
He tried to hide the miserable little creature

under his cloak, but she barked incessantly and chewed his beard. Then she threw up her yesterday's soup, and finally she had puppies in his lap.

Nothing very important in the way of production resulted from all the lady's literary activity. The verses of Sulpicia, if Sulpicia's they be, are the sole surviving evidence of creative effort among her kind; and, respectable as they are, they need not disturb Sappho's repose. It was indirectly that the Roman lady affected literature, since kinds began to be produced to her special taste; for it is hardly an accident that the *vers de société* should expand and the novel originate in periods when for the first time women were a large element in the reading public. If however we consider the main body of Latin literature with an eye to the reflection in it of the lady, we find at once one of the profound differences that contrast it with the literature of Greece. The feminism of the Greek is not here. Beyond any other literature we have, that of Rome is masculine. As Cornelia is pretty nearly an isolated case in Roman history, selected for a type because she is so far from typical, so Dido stands practically alone in Latin literature as a woman sympathetically drawn. Vergil, the most Hellenised of Romans, owes a very considerable part of his great prestige to the fact that he achieved the solitary love-story of Latin poetry. But even Vergil did not venture to make his heroine a Roman lady; and her regrettable lack of self-control served but to emphasise the hard core of Roman temperament in the hero. Lavinia was what a Roman always felt a woman should be; a somewhat cold embodiment of the virtues most serviceable to men, and devoid of that charm which he deemed in early days unnecessary and in later days pernicious. Apart from Dido there is nothing in Latin letters that corresponds with the women of Greek tragedy or even with Homer's women. The comedians, beginning where Greek comedy left off, deal with "little" women; the few ladies of their scenes are but indifferently rendered. The lyrists sing of light loves, humorous and sensual loves, and of disillusion and fatigue. The husband appears as the conventional *mari* of literature, the somewhat fatuous government against which the wife and the lover are perpetually in brilliant opposition. The smouldering hostility between male and female of this strong-willed race breaks now and then into flame. Juvenal's nerves are set on edge by the "new woman" of his day just as Cato's had been three hundred years before. His indictment of her vices loses its effect by including her foibles and even her good points. He couples homicide with a taste for literature, superstition with an interest in public affairs, as alike reprehensible. Cicero's attack on Clodia, Catullus's simultaneous love and hate, Martial's sinister epigrams, are the most powerful expressions the Roman knew of his feelings toward woman. Imaginatively she did not touch him; practically she was a disturbing element. The writers of Rome have defamed the Roman lady as the French novelists have defamed the lady of France. Just as honest Frenchmen to-day tell an incredulous Anglo-Saxon world that there are French ladies of high degree who are pure and devoted, so the careful historian of Rome must constantly remind his reader that the city never lacked for blameless ladies. The two true inferences to be made from the prevailing literary tone are that the women of Rome were active-minded, impulsive and passionate, and that the men of Rome had a certain hardness of fibre that made them very generally anti-feminist.

Cicero was a kindly man, cultivated and thoughtful; his modest fortune and social position excused him from many of the faults of greater men, while the respect justly entertained for his talents and for his character (since all things are relative) gave him a wide range of acquaintance. It is interesting to note in the letters of such a man his reaction against feminism. Cicero was no contemner of women. He disapproved the seclusion of the Greek lady and had no wish to see it introduced at Rome, but he would have been glad to see a censor established who should teach men how to govern their wives properly. His own wife, Terentia, presented few problems. She seems to have been a rather uninteresting person with a fortune of her own, and uncertain health. The bulk of her husband's letters to her however are full of confidence and pet-names. He lived with her without substantial difference for nearly thirty years, and then his tone began to change. The later letters are merely formal notes, and the last of them is such, it has been said, as no gentleman would write to his housekeeper. His next step was to divorce his old wife, on what ground we do not know, and to marry the youthful Publilia to whom he was not much more civil. He dearly loved his daughter Tullia and suffered profoundly from her loss. But while he was still under its recent shadow he writes to Atticus: "Publilia has written to tell me that her mother, on the advice of Publilius, is coming to see me with him and that she will come with them if I will allow it: she begs me in many words of entreaty that she may be allowed to do so, and that I would answer her letter. You see what an unpleasant business it is. I wrote back to say that it would be even more painful than it was when I told her that I wished to be alone, and that therefore I did not wish her to come to see me at this time. I thought that, if I made no answer, she would come with her mother: now I don't think she will. For it is evident that her letter is not her own composition. Now this is the very thing I wish to avoid, which I see will occur—namely, that they will come to my house: and the one way of avoiding it is to fly away. I would rather not, but I must. I beg you to find out the last day I can remain here without being caught." *

Cicero's brother Quintus married Pomponia, a sister of Cicero's friend Atticus. Apparently he liked his sister-in-law no better than his wife. At any rate he writes of her to Atticus in terms that furnish a vivid little scene from the comedy of manners: "I now come to that last line of your letter written crossways, in which you give me a word of caution about your sister. The facts of the matter are these. On arriving at my place at Arpinum, my brother came to see me, and our first subject of conversation was yourself, and we discussed it at great length.

* Cicero's Letters, trans. by Shuckburgh.

After this I brought the conversation round to
what you and I had discussed at Tusculum, on
the subject of your sister. I never saw anything
so gentle and placable as my brother was on
that occasion in regard to your sister: so much
so, indeed, that if there had been any cause of
quarrel on the ground of expense, it was not
apparent. So much for that day. Next day we
started from Arpinum and lunched at Arcanum.
You know his property there. When we got
there Quintus said, in his kindest manner,
'Pomponia, do you ask the ladies in; I will invite the men.' Nothing, as I thought, could be
more courteous, not only in the actual words
but also in the intention. But she, in the hearing of us all, exclaimed, 'I am only a stranger
here!' The origin of that was, as I think, the
fact that Statius had preceded us to look after
the luncheon. Thereupon Quintus said to me,
'There, that's what I have to put up with every
day!' You will say, 'Well, what does that
amount to?' A great deal; and indeed she had
irritated even me: her answer had been given
with such unnecessary acrimony, both of word
and look. I concealed my annoyance. We all
took our places at table except her. However
Quintus sent her dishes from the table, which
she declined. In short I thought I never saw
anything better-tempered than my brother or

crosser than your sister: and there were many particulars which I omit that raised my bile more than they did that of Quintus himself." *

These tiresome ladies of Cicero's family were by no means votaries of the new culture; they were the surviving form of the simple *materfamilias*. Even on them the new conditions had worked, bringing migraine and irritable nerves; but they were reposeful in comparison with the women of the world, Clodia, Sempronia and their like, whose lives touched Cicero's. "Hysteria" begins to be spoken of in literature, and social history begins to belong to the pathology of fatigue.

There was at no time at Rome anything that could be called a feministic movement. No solidarity existed in the sex split by caste into classes that had no motive in common. The ladies from time to time organised to obtain legislation in their interests, but as far as we know such legislation dealt only with pecuniary questions. We have no record of any attempt on their part to improve the lot of women in general. Women in general were in fact submerged. An inspection of the literature and the inscriptions of the late Republic and the early Empire gives the odd impression that the Roman women of the lower classes had pretty

* Cicero's Letters, trans. by Shuckburgh.

nearly ceased to exist.   The professional woman,
if we may so call her, the doctor, the ac-
coucheuse, the masseuse, the actress, the dancer,
the courtesan, the dressmaker, was almost
always a Greek.   In trade and industry the
same was true; according to the inscriptions,
Greek women were the fishmongers, the bar-
maids and the laundresses of Rome.   No one
can doubt that hundreds of thousands of hard-
working, god-fearing Roman women lived silent, unrecorded lives, and bore children to carry
on the state.   But the lady had nothing to do
with them.   Her struggles were directed to the
strengthening of her own position.   It was to
this end that Hortensia and her ladies came
down to the forum to argue that taxation without representation is tyranny.   When the Second Triumvirate were driven to every expedi-
ent to find money for the war with Brutus and
Cassius they published an edict requiring fourteen hundred of the richest women to make a
valuation of their property and to furnish for
the war such portion as the triumvirs should
require from each.   A body of the women concerned forced their way to the tribunal of the
triumvirs in the forum—a thing no man durst do
in those days.   Hortensia, (daughter of the
great Hortensius, a leader of the bar, Cicero's

rival, Verres' counsel,) was their spokesman. Appian gives us her speech:

"As is befitting women of our rank addressing a petition to you, we had recourse to your female relatives. Having suffered unseemly treatment on the part of Fulvia, we have been compelled to visit the forum. You have deprived us of our fathers, our sons, our husbands and our brothers, whom you accuse of having wronged you. If you take away our property also, you reduce us to a condition unbecoming our birth. If we women have not voted you public enemies, have not torn down your houses or led an army against you, why do you visit upon us the same punishment as upon the guilty, whose offences we have not shared? Why should we pay taxes when we have no part in the honours, the commands, the statecraft for which you contend? 'Because this is a time of war,' do you say? Let war with the Gauls or the Parthians come, and we shall not be inferior to our mothers in zeal for the common safety; but for civil wars may we never contribute."

"When Hortensia had thus spoken," says Appian, "the triumvirs were angry that women should dare to hold a public meeting when the men were silent. They ordered the lictors to drive them away from the tribunal, which they proceeded to do until cries were raised by the multitude outside, when the lictors desisted and the triumvirs said they would postpone till the next day the consideration of the matter. On the following day they reduced the number of women from fourteen hundred to four hundred." *

Public speaking had no terrors for the Roman lady. We read of women of litigious temperament who were constantly at law, and who argued their own cases in the prætor's court and in the forum. The practice was prevalent enough to need an edict to suppress it. Business on a large scale sometimes provided an outlet for the energies of the restless, able and idle *domina*. The manufacture of bricks seems to have been largely in her hands, for almost every Roman brick is stamped with the name of its maker, and the names of many great ladies, including even empresses, are handed down to us on the remnants of their product.

* Appian, trans. by Horace White.

III

THE great field, however, for the activity of the Roman lady was the exertion of her personal influence and the development of her power in political and social intrigue. The amorous intrigue, for which she is perhaps most famous, should be subordinated to the other two, for it was apparently in many cases their handmaid. Like the male of her kind the Roman lady was possessed of great sexual excitability and she indulged it as freely as he. In her case as in his, love turned easily to hate and even more easily to ennui. Like him, while indulging passion she despised its object. Like him, she judged power and money to be the great goods. Clodia and Sempronia are men in petticoats; they have the hot blood and the cool heads of men; their loveliness is the poisoned weapon with which they carry on the sex war.

The tendency towards concentration of power in the hands of two or three men gave the Roman lady a more dazzling opportunity. Nero wished that the people had but one neck; the lady's more reasonable desire was attained when the governing power had but one heart. The women of the Triumvirates are hardly less striking figures than the men. The empire saw a succession of masterful women, indistinguishable psychologically from the male. Augustus caused public honours to be accorded to his wife and to his sister. Tacitus was struck by the significant novelty of a woman enthroned when Agrippina was seated near Claudius to review a Roman army. With the Antonines titles for women began to develop, "mother of the legions," "mother of the senate and the people." It was debated in the senate whether magistrates sent to govern the provinces should be permitted to take their wives with them, and in the course of the discussion conservative opinion declared that the official ladies were altogether too active in political matters. The governor's wife was a force. All the intrigues of the province centred in her; she had her finger in every pie; even military discipline got into her department. She would appear on horseback beside her husband, inspect drill, and harangue the troops. Many a sturdy Roman seems to have felt towards this efficient lady as the Rev. Mr. Crawley felt towards Mrs. Proudy, and to have said as he did, "Woman, the distaff were more fitting for you!"

The great lady of the empire was aware that the splendour of her position placed her above criticism, or at any rate above any painful results from it, and this consciousness reinforced the tendency she had always had to let herself go. Very far indeed she went. As in the case of the man of her kind, very brutal pleasures and very crude vice were needed to stimulate her nerves. It was an extraordinary age and produced many phenomena that belong to the department of pathology. Its moralists delighted to paint its blackness; but in more cases than one the moralists knew by hearsay only of the wickedness of great ladies, being themselves surrounded by pure and gentle women.

It is very plain that the Roman resented and dreaded the development in his womankind of the desire to please. The old Roman lady, according to tradition, had entertained no such desire. She rested, like a man, on her sterling qualities. To be charming was, in Roman eyes, an admission both of weakness and of ambition. Unless a woman wanted something she ought not to have, she had no need of charm; and if she stooped to its use it must be because she had not the force of brains and character to reach her end by more manly means. Why did an honest woman wish to be attractive? Whom should she attract but her husband, who, by hypothesis, was sufficiently attracted already? Tacitus says of Livia that "she was more gracious in manners than would have been approved in a woman of the olden time." The rhetor Porcius Latro declared that a lady who wished to be safe from insulting advances should bestow only so much care on her toilet as not to be dirty. She should be accompanied by elderly maidservants whose respectability would warn off the enterprising. She should walk with downcast eyes, and if she met a pertinacious admirer, she should be rude rather than encouraging. But such (said he) was not the conduct of women of the world. They ran to meet temptation. Their faces were arranged for seduction, their bodies were just covered and that was all, their talk was charming and witty, and their manner was so caressing that any man dared approach them.

The Roman lady had in fact discovered the smokeless powder that put her on a somewhat less unequal military footing with the enemy. Social changes in Rome had brought her from the privacy of her own house into the world of society. She found herself at the head of a great establishment, with town-house and country-house, with a round of magnificent entertainment to offer and to receive, and with more money to spend than Europe had ever seen collected before or would see again for many centuries. Supposing her singly devoted to her husband, she found she could be of immense assistance to his career. Often, too, she found that she must compete with other women for his admiration. An attractive *demi-monde*, chiefly Greek, had become an institution in Rome. It behooved a wife to be as charming and as intelligent as the ladies without the pale. The art of fascination once learned, it was difficult not to keep it in practice at the expense of the first comer. And when a woman had discovered that she counted for something in her husband's career, she not unnaturally aspired to a career of her own. Seneca expressed succinctly the dilemma in which the Roman found himself: it is hard, said he, to keep a wife whom everyone admires; and if no one admires her it is hard to have to live with her, yourself.

We have a great deal of detailed information about the ladies of Rome. Many are known to us by name, and we are aware of the impression they made on their contemporaries. We should not be helped in differentiating them from other ladies by opening a ledger and setting down the good against the bad, Calpurnia against Faustina and Alcmene against Trimalchio's wife. The trait that is interesting for our purpose is present in good and bad alike. The Roman lady was a person; indeed, she was often what we call a "character." She is distinguished from the Athenian lady as a statue in the round is distinguished from a relief.

Once for all she was detached from the background of family life and, not supported
throughout her height by the fabric of society,
must see to it that her personal centre of gravity
should not lie without her base. She committed her own sins and bore her own punishment.
Her virtues were her own and did not often
take the direction of self-effacement. The
strong men among whom she lived, who broke
everything else, could not break her.

THE LADY ABBESS

I

"Set a price on thy love. Thou canst not name so much but I will give thee for thy love much more."—ANCREN RIWLE.

THE economic paradox that confronts women in general is especially uncompromising for the lady. In defiance of the axiom that he who works, eats, the lady who works has less to eat than the lady who does not. There is no profession open to her that is nearly as lucrative as marriage, and the more lucrative the marriage the less work it involves. The economic prizes are therefore awarded in such a way as directly to discourage productive activity on the part of the lady. If a brother and sister are equally qualified for, let us say, the practice of medicine, the brother has, besides the scientific motive, the economic motive. The ardent pursuit of his profession will if successful make him a rich man. His sister on the other hand will never earn absolutely as much money as he, and relatively her earnings will be negligible in comparison with her income if she should marry a millionaire. But if she be known to have committed herself to the study of medicine her chance of marrying a millionaire is practically eliminated.

Apart from the crude economic question, the things that most women mean when they speak of "happiness," that is, love and children and the little republic of the home, depend upon the favour of men, and the qualities that win this favour are not in general those that are most useful for other purposes. A girl should not be too intelligent or too good or too highly differentiated in any direction. Like a ready-made garment she should be designed to fit the average man. She should have "just about as much religion as my William likes." The age-long operation of this rule, by which the least strongly individualised women are the most likely to have a chance to transmit their qualities, has given it the air of a natural law. Though the lady has generally yielded it unquestioning obedience, she often dreams of a land like that of the Amazons, where she might be judged on her merits instead of on her charms. Seeing that in the world a woman's social position, her daily food, her chance of children, depend on her exerting sufficient charm to induce some man to assume the responsibility and expense of maintaining her for life, and that the qualities on which this charm depends are sometimes altogether unattainable by a given woman, it is not surprising that exceptional women are willing to eliminate from their lives the whole question of marriage and motherhood, for the sake of a free development irrespective of its bearing on the other sex.

No institution in Europe has ever won for the lady the freedom of development that she enjoyed in the convent in the early days. The modern college for women only feebly reproduces it, since the college for women has arisen at a time when colleges in general are under a cloud. The lady-abbess on the other hand was part of the two great social forces of her time, feudalism and the church. Great spiritual rewards and great worldly prizes were alike within her grasp. She was treated as an equal by the men of her class, as is witnessed by letters we still have from popes and emperors to abbesses. She had the stimulus of competition with men in executive capacity, in scholarship and in artistic production, since her work was freely set before the general public; but she was relieved by the circumstances of her environment of the ceaseless competition in common life of woman with woman for the favour of the individual man. In the cloister of the great days, as on a small scale in the college for women to-day, women were judged by each

other, as men are everywhere judged by each
other, for sterling qualities of head and heart
and character. The strongest argument against
the coeducational college is that the presence
of the male brings in the factor of sexual selec-
tion, and the girl who is elected to the class-
office is not necessarily the ablest or the wisest
or the kindest, but the possessor of the longest
eyelashes. The lady does not often rise to the
point of deciding against sex. The choice
is a cruel one, and in the individual case the rewards of the ascetic course are too small and
too uncertain. At no other time than the aristocratic period of the cloister have the rewards
so preponderated as to carry her over in numbers. In studying this interesting phenomenon
we must divest our minds of the conventional
picture of the nun. The Little Sister of the
Poor is the product of a number of social motives that had not begun to operate when the
lady-abbess came into being. In fact her day
is almost over when the Poor Clares appear.
Her roots lie in a society that is pre-feudal,
though feudalism played into her hand, and in
a psychology that is pre-Christian, though she
ruled in the name of Christ.

The worship of Demeter the mother-goddess
which was one of the central facts of Greek religious life spread and flourished in the west.

Sicily, the granary of the ancient world, became naturally in legend the scene of the rape of Persephone and of the wanderings of her mother, the giver of grain to men. The Romans adopted the worship of this ancient hypostasis of woman's share in primitive culture, ranging it beside the cult of their own Bona Dea and sometimes confusing the two. Catana was one of the places where the great festivals of the Lesser and the Greater Eleusinia were celebrated in spring and autumn with high devotion and with all the pomp of the rubric. The main features of the festival were everywhere the same; the carrying on a cart through the streets of the symbolic pomegranate and poppy-seed, the great procession walking with torches far into the night to typify the search of the goddess for her child, the mumming, the ringing of bells, the exhibition of the sacred veil, the mystic meal of bread for the initiate and the mystic pouring out of wine. At Catana, as Ovid tells us, these customary elements of the feast were supplemented by a horse-race.

Miss Eckenstein (to whose important *Woman under Monasticism* I am indebted at every turn) calls attention to the description given early in the last century by the English traveller Blunt of the festival of Saint Agatha as he saw it in

Catania and, I may add, as it is celebrated there to this day. It begins with a horse-race and its chief event, next to the mass, is a great procession, lasting into the night, in which the participants carry torches and ring bells as they follow a waggon which bears the relics of the saint, among them her veil and her breasts, torn off by her persecutors. The saint has two festivals yearly, one in the autumn and one in the spring. It remains to point out that though it is disputed whether the breasts were or were not part of the ancient ritual, they are a likely enough symbol of exuberance. Also, "Agatha" is the Greek word for "Bona," and does not occur as a proper name before the appearance of the saint. But the Acta Sanctorum knows all about Saint Agatha, a Christian virgin and martyr of Catania in the third century, and is able to give full details of her parentage and history, adding that her fame spread at an early date into Italy and Greece.

The process here visible went on everywhere as Christianity spread in Europe. The places, the persons and the ritual of heathen worship were taken in bodily by the new religion with a more or less successful effort at assimilation. Not only the classic cults of Greece and Rome but the cruder religions of the barbarians of the north were to be conciliated. And in all of these, classic and crude alike, the old status of woman was abundantly reflected. A purely patriarchal religion would not serve; the Virgin and the female saints became more and more necessary to bridge the chasm. It is not by accident that the festivals of the Virgin so often coincide with those of heathen deities, for in the seventh century Pope Sergius ordered that this should be so as a matter of policy. In the long centuries needed for the Christianising of Europe, heathendom reacted powerfully on the new faith. Local saints everywhere are its work. In the early days a saint needed not to be canonised by Rome; it was necessary only that he should be entered in a local calendar, and the local calendar was in the hands of local dignitaries of the church. Under pressure of popular demand every sacred place in heathendom bade fair to have its saint, and many of these improvised saints were gradually fitted out with legends and historical relations. It was not until the twelfth century that Rome felt that the process had gone far enough and withdrew the power of canonisation into her own hands.

Although the German tribes were already patriarchal in organisation when they came in contact with the Romans, they carried abundant evidence in their traditions, their customs and their cults of an earlier social system. The queen of saga and of history, the tribal-mother with her occult powers and her status of priestess to goddesses who were also tribal, the recognised existence of certain bodies of women outside the family, are all survivals of the mother-age with its primitive culture and social organisation. With these various phenomena the church dealt in various ways: roughly we may say that the tribal goddess she used as a saint, the priestess she banned as a witch; the unattached woman she segregated under a somewhat summary classification as either nun or castaway. There seems to be no doubt that we must regard the immense popularity of the convent in Europe in early times as largely due to the uneasiness of women under a patriarchal régime. We think to-day of the cloister as a refuge from the distracting liberty of secular life; it seems paradoxical and yet it is apparently true that the women of early Christendom fled from the constraint of home to the expansion of the cloister. Under patriarchalism the problem of the unassigned woman becomes one of considerable perplexity to herself and to society. A stigma is attached to her which acts as a detriment to rebels in the ranks. The "loose," i. e., the unattached, woman is sharply marked off from the lady, so that the choice lies between the constraints of social and economic dependence on the one hand and social outlawry on the other. These considerations account for the fact that the nun of early northern Christianity was by no means a type of self-effacement but was often a spirited and sometimes a lawless person, and that the abbess was more generally than not a woman of good birth, strong character and independent ways. Sometimes she had tried marriage, sometimes she had condemned it without a trial. It offered little scope for the free development of women, but there were many women insisting on free development. To such the convent was a godsend, and we may almost say that the lady-abbess is the successor of the saga-heroine. Monasticism as the Eastern world practised it was by no means congenial in general to the Frankish habit of mind. The worn-out races embraced it as a refuge from the growing difficulties of life with which they had no longer energy to cope. The fresh races on the other hand had an immense amount of the will to live to work off before they in their turn should dwindle toward self-effacement, abnegation and the meeker virtues. The men among the Franks felt no call to the cloister. There is small record of Frankish princes entering the convent of their free will. For men the world was too full of opportunity. But maidens, wives and widows of the royal house joined religious communities, not because they were spiritually unlike their men, but because they were like them. The impulse toward leadership which kept the men in the world sent the women out of it. Radegund, founder of the convent of Poitiers, was fifth among the seven recognised wives of King Clothair. She was a princess of the untamed Thuringians, whom Clothair captured with her brother on one of his raids into the eastern wilds. She was a person of great spirit and perfect personal courage. She was the sort of woman (her biographers say) who keeps her husband's dinner waiting while she visits the sick, and annoys him by her open preference for the society of learned clerks. When finally she made up her mind to leave her husband she fastened upon an unhappy prelate, Bishop Medardus of Noyon, the dangerous task of sealing her from the world. "If you refuse to consecrate me," she said grimly, "a lamb will be lost to the flock." The bishop quailed before the lamb and Radegund entered the life at Poitiers that gave play to her great powers of organisation, diplomacy and leadership. Her nuns were her true spiritual children. After her death two rival claimants for the office of abbess contended even with violence. Leubover was the regularly appointed successor, but Chrodield, daughter and cousin of kings, heading a faction attacked and put to flight the clerics who excommunicated her party. Gregory of Tours tells how Chrodield, having collected about her a band of murderers and vagrants of all kinds, dwelt in open revolt and ordered her followers to break into the nunnery at night and forcibly to bear off the abbess. But the abbess, who was suffering from a gouty foot, on hearing the noise of their approach asked to be carried before the shrine of the Holy Ghost. The rebels rushed in with swords and lances, and, mistaking in the dark, the prioress for the abbess, carried her off, dishevelled and stripped of her cloak. The bishops were afraid to enter Poitiers and the nuns kept the district terrorised until the king sent troops to reduce them. Only after the soldiers had actually charged them, cutting them down with sword and spear, was the neighbourhood at peace. It was not with these ladies in mind that Wordsworth found the sunset-hour as "quiet as a nun."

The women-saints of England are all Anglo-Saxon; after the coming of the Normans there are no more of them. And these early saints were generally ladies of high degree. Hilda, the famous abbess of Whitby, was grandniece of Edwin, king of Northumbria. The first religious settlement for women in England was founded by Enswith, daughter of Edbald, king of Kent. This Christian princess was sought in marriage by a heathen king of Northumbria whom she challenged to prove the power of his gods by inducing them miraculously to lengthen a beam. The suitor failed and withdrew. Enswith herself without difficulty caused a stream to flow up hill. Bede's statement that the ladies of his day were sent to the continent to be educated is borne out by what we know of Saint Mildred, abbess of Upminster in Thanet. She was sent as a girl to Chelles, where, among other adventures, she was cast by the abbess into a burning furnace for contumacy but escaped unhurt. When she returned to England she stepped from the vessel upon a flat stone which retained the print of her feet. Nay, more, says her chronicler: "the dust that was scrapen off thence being drunk did cure sundry diseases." A blood-fine being due her from Egbert, king of Kent, she was promised as much land as her deer could run over in one course, and the animal covered ten thousand acres of the best land in Kent.

We obtain a glimpse of the culture of the Anglo-Saxon nun by consulting the correspondence of St. Boniface, the friend of many cloistered ladies. They write to him in fluent Latin on many different subjects; one sends him some hexameter verses, another sends him fifty gold-pieces and an altar-cloth. One says, "I prefer thee almost to all others of the masculine sex in affectionate love;" another "salutes her revered lover in Christ;" yet another says, "I shall always cling to thy neck with sisterly embraces." Like other priests in all ages the good bishop is greatly comforted in times of discouragement by the affection of his feminine admirers. He begs one of them to finish the copy of the epistles of Peter which she had begun to write for him in letters of gold. He responds to all their philandering with advice and sentiment and little presents. The noble Edburga, abbess of a house in Devonshire which she freely left to reside in Rome, is "his dearest lady and in Christ's love to be preferred to all others of the female sex." Nevertheless he does not approve of continental travel for Anglo-Saxon nuns, and writes to Cuthbert of Canterbury: "I will not withhold from your holiness that it were a good thing if the synod and your princes forbade women, and those who have taken the veil, to travel and stay abroad as they do. For there are very few districts of Lombardy in which there is not some woman of Anglian origin living a loose life among the Franks and the Gauls. This is a scandal and disgrace to your whole church."

The composite photograph of the correspondents of Boniface shows a lady as important as a man, as well educated and as economically free as a man, thoroughly understanding the politics of her time and taking a hand in them, standing solidly on her own feet and sweetening existence with the harmless sentimentalism so much used by men. She has contrived that love, if not banished from her life, should be a thing apart, not her whole existence.

The foundation of great abbeys like Thanet and Ely, Whitby and Barking, was the result of the Anglo-Saxon social organisation which allowed women in some cases to hold real property, just as the existence of the female saint was due to the Teutonic estimate of the personal value of women. After the social ideas of the Normans became dominant, there were in England no more women-saints and few more abbeys for women were founded. The new settlements for religious women after the conquest were generally priories, and the prioress was of very inferior importance to the abbess. But though the abbess owed her existence to an earlier social system, she was rather strengthened than weakened by the application to her case of feudal principles. Being always a landlord and sometimes a very great one, she shared the prestige of the land-lord class. She was in some cases of such quality as to hold of the king "by an entire barony." By right of tenure she had the privi-lege at one period of being summoned to parliament. She drew two incomes, spirituali-ties from the churches in her jurisdiction and temporalities from her lands. Her manors often lay in several different shires, at a con-siderable distance from the abbey. It was pro-fanely said that if the abbot of Glastonbury were to marry the abbess of Shrewsbury, their heir would own more land than the king. This abbess had in her gift several prebends; in the reign of Henry I she found seven knights for the king's service, and she held her own courts for pleas of debts and the like. The great capacity for business necessary to conduct the affairs of so complex a position seems to have been possessed by the average abbess, for the property of the old houses at the time of the dissolution was in a very flourishing condition.

Among the Saxons on the continent the aristocratic tone of the convent was fully as marked. Whole families of royal princesses took the veil, rather gaining the world than losing it by the step. As in England, the abbess was virtually a baron. She was overlord often of an immense property, holding directly from the king. Like a baron she had the right of ban, she sent her contingent of armed knights into the field, she issued the summons to her own courts, she was summoned to the Reichstag, and in some instances she struck her own coins. The abbess was in close relations with the court and imperial politics. Matilda abbess of Quedlinburg was twice regent for her nephew Otto III, dealt strongly in that capacity with the invading Wends and summoned a diet on her own authority.

Under the presidency of great ladies of this type the abbeys everywhere before the twelfth century were centres where the daughters of nobles might live a pleasant life and receive such education as the time afforded. The early nun was not even in form what we commonly think of by that name. She was not always bound by vows, nor distinguished by her habit, nor even required to live in a particular place. Originally she as often as not remained in the world though dedicated to God. When she was attached to a convent it was difficult to find means to constrain her to stay in it. We have seen how Boniface wrote to Cuthbert on this subject. Eldhelm in the eighth century describes thus the dress of the nuns of his time: "A vest of fine linen of a violet colour is worn, above it a scarlet tunic with a hood, sleeves striped with silk and trimmed with red fur; the locks on the forehead and the temples are curled with a crisping-iron, the dark head-veil is given up for white and coloured head-dresses which, with bows of ribbon sewn on, reach down to the ground; the nails, like those of a falcon or sparrow-hawk, are pared to resemble talons." Bede records of the abbey of Coldringham that "the virgins who are vowed to God, laying aside all respect for their profession, whenever they have leisure spend all their time in weaving fine garments with which they adorn themselves like brides." A twelfth century document shows that at that time in Bavaria, Benedictine nuns went about as freely as monks, and wore no distinctive dress.

The phenomenon of the "double monastery" formed in early days a deviation from the nunnery as we think of it. From the necessity of having priests at hand to minister spiritually to religious women, it seemed reasonable to make houses for nuns side by side with houses for monks, among whom there were always a certain number in orders. The problem that resulted was one of perpetual difficulty. How were the women to get just what they needed from the

men and no more? St. Basil in his double
monastery in Pontus had already been perplexed
by difficult questions. May the head of the
monastery (he asks) speak with any virgins
other than the head of the sisters? When a
sister confesses to a priest should the mother of
the monastery be present? In Europe the
double monastery was very popular; "a chorus
of athletes of God and of chaste virgins," an
early writer rapturously calls it. Architectural
remains show us the various shifts different
communities were put to, that unity and isolation might be harmonised, as in a hospital devoted to both diphtheria and small-pox. Often
there were two churches in the monastery, one
for the men and one for the women; but sometimes a common church was split by a wall just
high enough to prevent the congregation on
one side from having sight of the other. The
two sets must not be able to talk with each other,
—their voices might mingle only in "recitation,
song, groans or sighs." The two houses were
often separated by a common cemetery, for in
death there is neither male nor female. In
Spain it was permitted to certain monks to kiss
the hand of certain nuns in greeting, but the
occasions for this observance are strictly regulated. By the rule of St. Fructuosus it is laid
down that if a monk fall ill he must not lie in

a monastery of nuns, lest his soul grow sick while his body grows well. Monk and nun may not eat together. An odd form of double monastery was especially common in Spain and in England, where a whole family would transform itself into a religious house, father and mother, children and servants, continuing to live together in their old relations with the new ones added. The motive in most cases seems to have been pecuniary; hereditary possessions could in this way be safeguarded by royal charter and the prestige of religion. Sometimes the husband did not himself take the tonsure but merely had his wife made an "abbess."

In many of the double monasteries an abbess was at the head of all, both men and women. It was not unnatural that she should now and then try to exceed the limits set by the church to the services of women. Sometimes she heard confession and occasionally she excommunicated. Sometimes she was "weighed down with anxiety for the account she will have to give at the day of judgment for her government of a cloister containing men and women of various ages." All the early nunneries in England of which we have any evidence on the point were of this type, and without exception the whole establishment was ruled over by a woman. The

most famous example is of course Hilda of
Whitby, great lady, administrator, theologian,
educator and saint. We know very little of the
personal character of these women; the records
are confined for the most parts to their important acts of policy, their correspondence with
princes and bishops and the miracles they
wrought. Every mention of them however
carries an intimation of the aristocratic character of the profession. When the monk became an object of contempt at court, the nun
was still in fashion. Her social position kept
pace with that of the secular clergy rather than
with that of her brother regulars. Her schools
were for the daughters of gentlefolk; to have
been bred in a convent was a mark of caste.

The coign of vantage from which the nunnery was able to despise the world was however not merely that of aristocratic association.
A religious house was generally the home of
order and regularity in a world of confusion
and a point of light in a twilit age. If St.
Benedict had done nothing more than establish
the eight daily canonical hours, he would have
been a benefactor of Europe. The great moral
value of regular hours is everywhere admitted
to-day and is built upon in the army, in the
"rest-cure," in ships at sea, as well as in private
life. When the prodigal determines to turn

over a new leaf he is pretty sure to have his watch regulated as one of the preliminary steps. The great superiority in social organisation among men as compared with women is reflected in the fact that their watches are more apt to be right. The monastery has from the first with a sure instinct of self-preservation clung to the observance of the hours as the core of its life, and the rest broken by matins, lauds and prime, has been made good by the mental repose secured through the twenty-four hours by accurate and minute division of time and frequent change of occupation.

On the productive side, the nun of the centuries before the twelfth is popularly best known by her artistic weaving and needlework. Scanty as are the remains of her art they bear out to the full the praise lavished upon it by the old writers. In early times the blind walls of the basilica offered space for large hangings; when Gothic architecture removed the motive for these, the nuns concentrated upon vestments and the furniture of the altar. The famous cope of Syon, probably the handiwork of nuns, shows the excellence in design as well as in execution of early English work. Sometimes sentiment would allow an abbess to prepare a winding-sheet for a friendly abbot during his lifetime. So little do the fundamental ideas of men concerning life and death vary from age to age and from land to land, that Penelope of Ithaca expressed her respect for her husband's father by the weaving of the famous web that was to be his shroud, precisely as an abbess of Repton wrought a winding-sheet for St. Guthlac, and an abbess of Whitby prepared one for Cuthbert of Lindisfarne. Nor did the good ladies always confine their work to pious aims. One of the charges of the rebellious Chrodield against the abbess of Poitiers was that she made a robe for her niece out of part of an altar-cloth. A Council of the eighth century decides that "time shall be devoted more to reading books and to chanting psalms than to weaving and decorating clothes with various colours in unprofitable richness."

But it would be a mistake to suppose that the life of the cloistered lady was divided between devotion and needlework. As far as the records go they show that she was free to try her hand at almost anything. Many a famous scribe developed in the nunnery, scholar and artist in one. Emo, abbot of a double Premonstrant house, not only encouraged his clerks to write, acting as their instructor, "but taking account of the diligence of the female sex" he set women who were clever at writing to the assiduous practice of the art. Famous for centuries were the illuminated transcripts of Diemund of Wessobrunn and of Leukardis of Mallersdorf.

When the Germans bombarded Strasburg in 1870 they destroyed (among other things) the manuscript and the only complete copy of the *Garden of Delights,* the *magnum opus* of Herrad, abbess of Hohenburg. Fortunately transcripts or copies of parts of it survive and have been piously collected, giving us a very vivid little picture of social life in the twelfth century. Herrad's nuns, according to her own pictures of them, wore clothes differing but little from those of world's women. The only uniform article of dress was a white turban, over which the veil was thrown, but the veil itself might be red or purple while the dress was also various in colour and apparently subject to the wearer's taste. Herrad's great work was written for the instruction of her nuns, and covers the history of the world, based on the Bible narrative. She digresses frequently into questions of philosophy, ethics and profane learning. In discussing the decay of faith in connection with the Tower of Babel, she introduces a very respectful graphic presentation of the Seven Liberal Arts. Personified as women in twelfth century dress they are ranged around Philosophy, Socrates and Plato, and there is nothing to warn the nuns against their charms unless it be the head of a howling dog carried by Dialectic.

The interest taken in the nunnery in natural science may be seen by reference to the encyclopædic *Physics* of Hildegard, abbess of Rupertsberg, a complete *materia medica* of the middle age. Hildegard describes a large number of plants, animals and chemical substances, closing each description with a statement of the object's therapeutic qualities. We cannot say that her conclusions are always based on direct observation, for she has as much to say about the unicorn as about the pig. But she holds the sound conviction that "devils" can be eliminated from the system by water-drinking, and displays in general so much common-sense that it is clear her reputation for wonderful cures rested on a basis of scientific treatment. The care of the sick was always one of the duties of a religious house, where a light diet, regular hours and a generally pure water supply furnished better sanitary conditions than were always attainable in the world. Books such as those of Herrad and Hildegard presuppose a tradition of scientific interest, and the co-operation of intelligent pupils as well as the stimulus of an appreciative public. A good deal of the work in each was probably done, as we should say to-day, in the seminar, and it is fair to infer from them a widespread intellectual interest and freedom among the pupils in the cloister.

Gerberg, abbess of Gandersheim and daughter of Duke Lindolf, the progenitor of the royal house of Saxony, was an excellent scholar and encouraged among her nuns the studies she had herself followed under the guidance of learned men. In the scholarly atmosphere of her abbey in the tenth century the nun Hrotsvith produced the works which make her name memorable not only among women but in the general history of literature. Her metrical legends and history of her own time have merits of their own, but they can be paralleled among the writings of other authors of the period. Her unique value is as a writer of Latin drama. From the close of classic times to the crude beginnings of the miracle play, we know of no dramatic composition in Europe save the seven plays of Hrotsvith. The first of the humanists, she has left us a full account of her admiration for classical literature and her determination to make its glories serviceable to the pure in heart. After praising enthusiastically the work of Terence she says: "I have not hesitated to take this poet's style as a model, and while others honour him by perusing his dramas, I have attempted in the very way in which he treats of unchaste love among evil women, to celebrate according to my ability the praiseworthy chasteness of god-like maidens. In doing so, I have often hesitated with a blush on my cheeks, because the nature of the work obliged me to concentrate my attention on the wicked passion of illicit love and on the tempting talk of the amorous, against which we at other times close our ears."*

Blush or no blush, this cloistered lady succeeded, like the chaste Richardson eight hundred years later, in causing virtue to undergo adventures of the interesting character that Terence and Fielding supposed to be reserved for vice. She anticipates Anatole France in treating the redemption of Thais by Paphnutius; Christian maidens repulse pagan lovers; the tragedy of martyrdom and the most realistic comedy relieve each other. Three virgins persecuted by Diocletian attract the eye of their gaoler; with the prospect of speedy death before them they laugh with all their hearts at the spell put upon him whereby he mistakes the kitchen for their chamber and fondles in his madness the pots and pans. Very thoroughly and with the wide sweep that we are wont to call virile did this lady deal with

* Translated by Miss Eckenstein.

life and letters.   Not her cloister, but the polite world of her time, was her public.   As evidence of her continued prestige it is interesting to note that four hundred years after her death the Rhenish Celtic Society printed an edition of her dramas and secured copyright by taking out what is believed to be the first "privilege" issued by the Imperial Council.

II

THE many influences that worked together to change men's view of life during the later middle ages were all reflected in the career of the lady-abbess.   Feudalism had seen her become a baron, strong individually and with the strength of her class.   At times when intellectual interests prevailed, her leisure and resources had enabled her to take a manful part in the literary production and in the queer scientific investigation of her age.   Her artistic achievements were, within their range, of a high order.   But in her breast as well as in the hard old social framework that supported her, solvents were at work.   Considering under three of its aspects a force which had many more, we may say roughly that these solvents were in religion the rediscovery of Christianity which resulted in the foundation of the mendicant orders, in social philosophy the recognition of the submerged, and in literature mysticism and romance. All these ideas which were destined to give a wonderful new value to life were welcomed and furthered by the lady-abbess, who could not foresee that her decadence was to be one of their by-products.

The profane love against which Herrad's virgins and martyrs fought was of the simple old pagan type. No emotional element was present in the heroine's breast to bring these dramas over into the class of the problem play. But a very different conception of the love of men and women, one of the most profound psychological changes of the middle age, had become the motive of a graceful literature. When every lady in the world had her love song it must not be supposed that the abbess would be without one. The mysticism of chivalry used the same vocabulary as the mysticism of religion. The knight's service to his lady, long, patient and (theoretically) not too clamorous for reward was a type of the impassioned service of monk or nun. A "maid of Christ" asked Thomas de Hales to write her a song and received the "Love Rune," which with its lively lilt and gentle gaiety remains one of the glories of Middle English literature. Its drift can be gathered from an artless translation of two or three stanzas:

"The love of man lasts but an hour,
  Now he loveth, now is he sad.
Now will he smile, now will he glow'r;
  Now is he wroth, now is he glad.
His love is here, and now 'tis yonder;
  He loves till he hath had his will.
To trust him does not make him fonder;
  Who trusts him is a zany still.

"Where are Paris and Heleyne
  That were so fair and bright of bloom?
Vanished are those lovers twain
  With Dido out into the gloom.
Hector of the strong right hand
  And Cæsar, lord of words enow,
Have perishéd from out the land
  As speeds the arrow from the bow."

But the lord Christ is introduced as the most desirable of lovers:

"Here is the richest man in land,
  As wide as men speak with the mouth.
All are vassals of his hand,
  East and west and north and south.

Henry king of all England
Holds of him and bends the knee.
Maiden, this lord sends command
He would fain be known to thee."

The *Ancren Riwle* or Rule for Recluses describes in courtly allegory the wooing of a maiden by the Lord of Heaven: "There was a lady besieged by her foes within an earthly castle, and her land was all destroyed and herself quite poor. The love of a powerful king was however fixed upon her with such boundless affection that to solicit her love he sent his messengers one after the other, and often many together, and sent her trinkets both many and fair, and supplies of victuals and help of his high retinue to hold her castle. She received them all as a careless creature with so hard a heart that he could never get nearer to her love. What would'st thou more? He came himself at last and showed her his fair face, since he was of all men the fairest to behold, and spoke so sweetly and with such gentle words that they might have raised the dead from death to life. And he wrought many wonders and did many wondrous deeds before her eyes, and showed her his power and told her of his kingdom, and offered to make her queen of all that he owned.

But all availed him naught. Was not this surprising mockery? For she was not worthy to have been his servant. But owing to his goodness love so mastered him that he said at last: 'Lady, thou art attacked, and thy enemies are so strong that thou canst not without my help escape their hands that thou mayest not be put to a shameful death. I am prompted by love of thee to undertake this fight, and rid thee of those that seek thy death. I know well that I shall receive a mortal wound, but I will do it gladly to win thy heart. Now I beseech thee for the love I bear thee that thou love me at least after my death, since thou would'st not in my lifetime.' Thus did the king. He freed her of her enemies and was himself wounded and slain in the end. Through a miracle he arose from death to life. Would not that same lady be of an evil kind if she did not love him above all things after this?" *

The literary nuns of the Abbey of Helfta were themselves minnesingers. Spiritual love in all its aspects was their theme. Ecstacy expressed itself in strains as strongly figurative as the *Song of Solomon*. Transforming love made the cloister-life to glow. Visions became common among inspired nuns. Purity itself was impassioned. By the laws of chivalry the knight's

* Translated by Miss Eckenstein.

love for his lady was expressed in courtesy and kindness toward all the world. In the cloister also devotion to the great lover expressed itself in tenderness for men.

The great monastic expansion of the twelfth century took a long step toward democracy in the cloister. The problem of the unattached woman of the lower class had become a menace to society. The great orders of Fontevraud and Prémontré as well as many less famous were organised in the interest of the helpless of all classes and particularly of the lost woman. Of Fontevraud we are told that "the poor were received, the feeble were not refused, nor women of evil life, nor sinners, neither lepers nor the helpless." Thousands of women entered these orders. From a bull of 1344 it is to be inferred that there were at that time about four hundred settlements of Premonstrant nuns. All the women in these settlements were professed, and their lives were spent in constant labour, which ultimately brought worldly as well as moral profit. These orders spread rapidly and widely. They were in harmony with the general tendency of the age, both ideally and practically; for while they gave ease to the rising social conscience of the upper classes, they also helped the growth of skilled labour and trade organisation among the lower.

We can best realise the contrast between the old nunnery and the new by noting two specific cases in England. In the middle of the twelfth century Mary of Blois, daughter of King Stephen, was abbess of the ancient foundation of Romsey, associated with many other royal and noble ladies. Upon the death of her brother William she became heiress of the County of Boulogne. Henry II thereupon overrode her vows, brought her from the cloister and married her to Matthew, son of the count of Flanders, who thus became count of Boulogne. Mary's sister Matilda had a somewhat similar experience, and her convent breeding left her with a taste for letters and the ability to correspond in Latin with learned men. At the very time that these great ladies were exemplifying in Wessex the solidarity of interest between court and cloister, Gilbert of Sempringham was creating from humble beginnings his great settlements for the higher life and his dwellings for the poor and the infirm, for lepers and for orphans. Gilbert was the son of a Norman baron by an English woman of low degree. He was educated in France and studied the great orders of the continent, with the result that when his growing foundation came to need a rule he gave it one of wide eclecticism to meet the needs of canons and nuns, laybrothers and laysisters. The simple life was to be lived at Sempringham, and to this art and letters seemed to be inimical. The rule declared pictures and sculpture superfluous, and forbade the use of the Latin tongue unless under special circumstances. A prior ruled the men, three prioresses the women who were twice as numerous. The women performed the domestic work for the whole body, handing the men's meals through a hole in the wall with a turntable.

But the humanitarianism that inspired Gilbert reached Matilda too, in spite of her classical education. A famous anecdote describes her girt with a towel and washing the feet of lepers. Her hospital of St. Giles in the East was for long the most important institution of its kind in England. "Leprosy" was in the middle ages a summary term for many forms of disfiguring skin disease. Fear of contagion was a comparatively late motive for its isolation, which originated in its loathsomeness to the eye. The care of the leper became a typical good work. His miserable lot as an outcast constituted a special appeal to the new tenderness of heart, while his repulsiveness made his tendance an instrument for the new effort to be like Christ. Great ladies everywhere, generally convent-bred, renounced place and pleasure to serve the sick and the poor. Virchow remarks that the great family of the Counts of Andechs and Meran, famous for its philanthropy, practically extinguished itself by devotion. Its men joined the crusades or the church, its women entered the cloister, and after a few generations this powerful and widespread family perished of its virtues.

The mendicant orders, which realised what Plato had maintained, that he who is to serve society must have nothing of his own, held up an ideal absolutely at variance with the vested interests which the abbess had so ably administered. Side by side with the feudal strongholds of the church, the Poor Clares built their huts, bearing towards them somewhat the relation that the Salvation Army bears to a charitable millionaire. The Poor Clares had no time for culture and the arts. Love for God and man and the passion for service carried into the vow of poverty thousands of women from every class. Asceticism and silence were opposed as methods to comfort and scholarship. The ultimate deterioration of the mendicants did not come until they had induced the general change of ideas that was to be responsible for the Protestant Reformation.

The decay of the aristocratic monastery was doubtless a step in advance in the history of men, but it was a calamity for the lady, who was reduced to the old dilemma of the home or outlawry. Luther had a thoroughly Mohammedan notion of woman's status,—only as a wife and mother had she a right to exist. Her education became a matter of no importance and virtually ceased. Even Fuller, the worthy seventeenth century divine, who cannot be accused of a bias in favour of convents, said: "They were good she schools wherein the girls and maids of the neighbourhood were taught to read and work; and sometimes a little Latin was taught them therein. Yea, give me leave to say, if such feminine foundations had still continued, provided no vow were obtruded upon them, (virginity is least kept where it is most constrained,) haply the weaker sex, besides the avoiding modern inconveniences, might be heightened to a higher perfection than hitherto hath been attained."

Without accepting Fuller's epigram we may admit that the ideal of virginity was not always attained in the cloister; neither is justice always attained on the bench nor valour in the army. Many a prioress besides Chaucer's may have had for her motto "Amor vincit omnia." But the very persistence of the system would be strong evidence, if we had no other, that on the whole the cloister had the esteem of its contemporaries, and that the women who gave it tone were in general true to their calling, and made whole-heartedly the sacrifice in return for which they received freedom.

THE LADY OF THE CASTLE

I

"Nul, s'il n'est cortois et sages,
Ne puet riens d'amors aprendre."—

CHRÉTIEN DE TROYES.

THE lady's life, and even her character, are always sensibly modified by the house she lives in, and the house represents the social or economic requirements of the man of her class. The man shapes the house and the house shapes the lady. The Roman villa, ample, luxurious and open, built to house a complicated social life, began to disappear in Europe together with the *pax Romana,* and the restriction of space set in that necessarily accompanies fortification. The Roman *castella,* originally established only on the frontier, sprang up everywhere; in the fourth century France bristled with them. When the barbarians were finally in control, it was they in turn who fortified strong natural points, often selecting the very sites on which the Romans had built and retaining the Roman plan—an artificial mound of earth surrounded by a palisade and a ditch, and surmounted by a tower. In forming a picture of the mediæval castle we must banish the vision of the coquettish chateau of the Renaissance, the fortified manor like Azay-le-Rideau, and the fortified palace like Chambord. Many a good knight in the twelfth century housed his family, his servants and his men-at-arms under the single roof of his donjon. All castles agreed in certain features. They were surrounded by a strong wall, punctuated by towers and by a great gate flanked with towers and equipped with drawbridge and port-cullis. The gate gave access to the lower court. The inner court was in its turn enclosed by a fortified wall; in the inner court stood the heart of the castle, the donjon; and within the donjon dwelt the lady.

Windows and doors were eschewed in castle architecture. The ground floor of the donjon had no opening of any kind, the entrance being invariably on the first floor and reached by a gently inclined bridge, which was removed or destroyed in case of siege. The whole of the first floor was occupied by a single room, the famous "hall" of ballad and history. This room was round, square or polygonal, according to the shape of the tower. It was lighted grudgingly by a narrow window here and there, set at the end of a sort of tunnel bored through

a wall eight or ten feet thick, and it was warmed
by open fires of logs. In the English manor
there prevailed until the sixteenth, and even the
seventeenth, century the Homeric custom of the
central hearth without a chimney. The smoke
made its more or less leisurely way out of a hole
in the roof directly over the hearth. But in
France the Roman chimney, never altogether
abandoned, was in common use from the eleventh century onward, and developed early its
characteristic conical hood. The hall was often
paved with tiles of white stone encrusted with
black mastic, and on this flooring were spread
thick rugs. If the company sat freely on the
floor it was not because there were no chairs,
though they were not as numerous as in the Homeric house. But a row of coffers often stood
against the walls, and sometimes also there were
massive forms with backs, divided like choir
stalls; and sometimes there were lighter benches,
easily moved about. Kings and great lords had
fald-stools, like the one in which the abbess Herrad's picture shows Herod seated, but it was not
every simple castellan who owned one. The as-
perities of all these somewhat unconciliating
seats were tempered by rugs and cushions, but a
study of them explains why persons of the romances so frequently sat upon the bed. In the
first place, the bed of the lord and the lady stood

as often as not in the hall, opposite the fireplace. It was large and monumental; the frame was gilded, carved, inlaid with ivory. Cords stretched on the frame held a feather bed, which was covered with sheets of linen or silk. During the day the bed was shrouded with a rich spread of fur, or silk, or cloth of gold. It was surrounded by curtains, which made it a room within a room. Herrad shows us Solomon sleeping in all the glory of the twelfth century, with a night-light and as easy a posture as can be assumed by a sleeper who wears a crown.

With all its splendour, the presence of the bed in the hall is symbolic of the change wrought in manners by lack of space. Privacy was gone. From Homer's time the spacious Greek house, copied by the Romans, had contained a number of small bedrooms, so that everyone might have his own. The chateau changed all that. The lord and the lady slept in the hall. On the floor above lay their children and their guests, often enough in but two rooms, the women in one and the men in the other. At the head of each bed was a bar on which the occupant hung his clothes. In the morning he could reach them from where he lay and dress himself behind his curtains before getting out of bed. Outside his curtains was the public. It is often lamented by critics of mediæval morals that young men had, apparently, free access to the bedrooms of young women and that they so often sat down to talk upon a *lit paré*. It must be remembered in this connection that the mediæval bedroom offered hardly more privacy than the American sleeping-car.

On the third floor slept the servants and men-at-arms. On the ground floor were store-rooms and offices. The kitchen was generally a separate building. In the basement was the bath-room, primitive in appointments, but a necessary of life. If the baron and his wife dressed before getting out of bed, and contented themselves with washing face and hands before facing the world, they were nevertheless systematic bathers. On the one hand there are the romances, which speak of bathing almost as often as Homer does. The guest is welcomed with a bath; the weary man and the invalid are refreshed by it. The ceremonial bath of bride and bridegroom before marriage, and of the knight before taking arms, are but the symbolic use of a common custom. And, on the other hand, there are the remains in many an ancient tower of the room devoted to the bath and of the pipes that served it. However rude the mechanism, refinement was there. Often the bath was perfumed or medicated with herbs. "Give me a bath that has run twice," asks a fastidious knight. As in Homer, the care of the bath and its preparation for even men guests was the work of the daughters of a hospitable house.

Apart from the question of the bath, everyone —the lord and his lady, their children and their guests—washed hands several times a day. Before and after dinner it was an inevitable ceremony. In early days, apparently, it took place at fixed stands, where water ran from taps. Later, as in Homer, water was poured for guests as they sat at table. This ablution was very necessary, for the lady of the castle, like Homer's lady, had no fork. In short, the classical fondness for water, derived from the Greeks through the Romans, prevailed in the Middle Age. There were public baths in large towns, and there were bathing resorts. Only by degrees did cleanliness fade out of Europe, and dirt did not triumph until the Renaissance. In 1292 the *rôle de la taille* mentions twenty-six baths in Paris; under Louis the Fourteenth there were but two.

The walls and ceiling of the castellan's hall were not so richly decorated as those of the hall of Menelaus. Instead of plates of metal and of coloured glass the Middle Age used paint. *Peinte à flors* is the common epithet. The persistent tradition of the Roman villa showed itself in degenerate classical motives—grotesque

acanthuses and distorted foliage. Sometimes
the artist ventured on human figures, drawing
them in silhouette against a (generally) light
background. The whole decorative effect was
cheerful. On feast-days the walls were hung
with embroidered stuffs: not until the thirteenth
century with tapestry properly so called.

If the lady's house, in order to keep her safe,
was obliged to contract the space at her disposal,
she found expansion and light and air in the
garden. Without the wall, at the foot of the
castle hill, approached often by a postern of its
own, lay her open-air drawing-room. The
garden of the Middle Age was strictly architectural. Its symmetical plan, with orderly sub-
divisions, the presence of seats of stone or turf,
sculptured fountains and plants in tubs, gave it
the air of a house without a roof. It was
planted with regard to the bird's-eye view from
above, and as seen from the castle must have
looked like a carpet or a tiled pavement. The
labyrinth and other familiar motives of floor
decoration are found in garden plans. An important feature is always the fountain. Even
in Paradise, as figured in Jean de Berri's *Book
of Hours,* a beautiful Gothic fountain refreshed
our first parents. Trees were clipped to shape,
artificial mounds were raised, stiff hedges divided one room, so to speak, from another.

Before the end of the Middle Age gardening had become a curious art, almost Japanese. Wonders of grafting, dwarfing and forcing were accomplished. The first hot-house appeared early in the thirteenth century. Fruit trees were used freely in the garden; Charles the Fifth planted a thousand cherry-trees in an architectural setting at St. Pol. The most usual flowers were roses of various colours, lilies and other bulbs, common violets and a sort that needed to be taken indoors in winter, stocks, pinks, lavender, pansies and columbine. Many gardens had ponds stocked with edible or curious fish. In some, native and foreign birds were kept. Often a park was added, in which dwelt wild and tame animals. The modern zoological garden is the direct descendant of the garden of the castle. In this charming setting many and many a scene of the romances is enacted. The frowning donjon by itself would leave the feudal lady only half explained; it is in the garden that we must look for the expansion of some of her most characteristic traits.

The lady's own outward appearance is almost as well known to us as that of her house and garden. It is not necessary to believe that she was as uniformly blond as the romances assert; they prove only that the favourite type was grey-eyed, fair-haired, white-skinned, with rosy cheeks and scarlet lips.   Whatever her complexion, the lady's costume consisted of three main items.   Next her body she wore a chemise of fine linen, "white as a meadow-flower."   This garment had sleeves, and covered the wearer from chin to foot.   Sometimes the collar and cuffs were embroidered with gold, and were allowed to show.   Over the chemise she put on the *pelisson,* a garment made of fur, but covered within with linen and without with silk.   The *pelisson* was indispensable in winter, indoors as well as out; but in summer it would be excessive, and there is reason to believe that the fur substrate was then withdrawn, leaving the border as before.   Over the *pelisson* the lady wore the famous *bliaut,* the dress of half the saints in Christendom as we see them in sculpture or in stained glass.   The *bliaut* was sometimes straight and simple, giving the wearer the same apparent diameter at shoulder, waist and knee.   Sometimes it was confined by a broad cuirass that outlined the breast and hips.   For material she might choose among a variety of woollen stuffs or among silks of great beauty, ranging in weight from samite to *crêpe de Chine.*   In purple and scarlet, green and blue, the lady dressed, with often a thread of gold interwoven, and with fringes and braids of gold in plenty.   The climax of her costume was the girdle, fastened loosely about the waist and falling to the bottom of the *bliaut.* Gold and jewels often went to make it; their brilliancy accented the lines of the lady's body and called attention to every movement as she walked. Her hair was woven with ribbons into two long braids, which she pulled forward and allowed to hang in front. Out of doors she wore a mantle which might open either in front or at the side, and was capable of highly effective draping. It could be arranged to show as much or as little as the wearer desired of the costume beneath. Both sexes covered the head out of doors with the *chaperon,* a sort of peaked hood with a cape. And both sexes wore pointed heelless shoes of stuff or leather, often elaborately ornamented.

Such in appearance were the castle and the lady. Doubtless it would be absurd to represent the social status of the lady as the direct outcome of the architecture of her home, since both were in fact the outcome and expression of the life of the man of her class and time. But it is certain that the castle was the primary condition of that life, and that, where its interests clashed with those of the lady, hers had to give way. In her everyday life she perhaps gained as much from its limitations as she lost. If, for instance, the knight had wished as earnestly as did the Greek to seclude his womankind, he could not have

done it; the donjon admitted of no gyneceum.
Though the lady had no privacy, she suffered
no isolation.   Her place was in the hall, and in
the hall the life of the house was transacted.
Whatever interested her husband was discussed
in her presence.   If a neighbour rode over to
invite him to join a foray or a crusade, the lady
could not but know what was in the wind.   If
she lost in refinement she gained in education.
The life of her time was an open book before
her; she was free to form her opinion of men
and things and to make her personality count
for what it was worth.

But the really sinister effect upon the lady of
the castle and its lands was one that resulted
from their meaning rather than from their physical characteristics.   They were held by the
knight from his overlord on condition of the payment of rental in the form of military service.
Every acre of ground was valued in terms of
fighting-men, and only the knight in person
could be sure of rallying the quota and producing them when required.   If the knight died,
in harness or in his bed, and left a widow with
young children or a daughter as his sole heir,
there was a good chance that the rent would not
be paid.   The overlord had the right, in view
of his interests in the matter, to see that a fief
should not be without a master; in other words,

to marry as soon as might be the widow or the
daughter of the deceased to some stout knight
who was willing to take the woman for the sake
of the fief.

"One of these days," says the king in *Char-
roi de Nîmes* to a baron who is threatening him,
"one of these days one of my peers will die; I
will give you his fief and his wife, if you will
take her." In fact, it could be said of the lady as
truly as of the serf that she "went with the land."
She knew this full well herself. In the romance
of *Girars de Viane* the Duchess of Bourgogne
came to the king, saying: "My husband is dead,
but of what avail is mourning? Give me a
strong man to my husband, for I am sore
pressed to defend my land." Young girls came
quite simply on the same errand. Helissent,
daughter of Yon of Gascony, presented herself
before Charlemagne and all his court with this
practical statement: "Two months ago my father
died; I am come to ask for a husband." Far-
seeing men betrothed or even married their children in infancy. Hardy younger sons might win
castle and lands by recommending themselves
through feats of arms to fathers of daughters.
Thus the aged Aimeri, in the *Enfans Aimeri,*
wished to provide for his sons by marriage. To
Garin he said: "Go to Bavaria and bid the Duke
Naimes to give you his daughter, with the city

of Anseiine, it harbours and shores. It is true this land is at the moment in the hands of the Saracens, but you have only to take it from them." Garin makes his way to Bavaria, and explains his idea to the duke. "You are of high race," answers the duke, "and I will give you my daughter of the fair face." He called for her forthwith. "Belle," said he, "I have given you a husband." "Blessed be God!" said the damsel.

In one aspect or another the identification of the fief and the lady provides the motive of a hundred chansons. It is the basis of her social importance, superseding the production of legitimate offspring, which was the basis of her social importance in Greece and, theoretically at any rate, in Rome. It would, perhaps, be paradoxical to say that a baron would prefer to be sure that his tenure was secure than that his son was legitimate, but it is certain that the relative value of the two things had shifted. The rehabilitation of the bastard was well under way, and formed a class of which we may perhaps consider that a man like Dunois was the culmination. It is far from paradoxical to say that, as a sort of indemnification for the iron hand laid upon her destiny by the system of land-tenure in the Middle Age, the lady achieved a new measure of personal liberty. She might within reason philander where she would, provided she married where she was bid.

The lady's education was probably, on the academic side at least, considerably better than her husband's. Very likely she could more often read and write than he. But, as in Homeric days, the want of reading was supplied for man and woman alike by the accomplishments of the *rhapsode,* who is now called a *jongleur.* Old and young, masters and servants, gathered after dinner in the hall to hear the deeds of princes, or love-songs, or the lives of the saints, according to the taste of the audience or the gift of the minstrel. It is hard to realise how uniform must have been the view of life, which was acquired not by private reading, but in groups from a conventional source. Such as it was, it was alike for both sexes. Not only in literary but in practical matters the daughter of the castle would receive much the same education as Helen of Troy. She would be a famous spinster and needlewoman, able to make a shirt or an altar-cloth. She would sit by the hour among her damsels in hall or in garden, developing stitch by stitch that incredible faculty of patience which alone has enabled the lady of all times to live with health and without too much analysis her life of constant suspension on the acts of another. All household work was familiar to her. Life was full of emergencies, and she was ready for them. Often she was a skilful leech, unafraid of blood, trained to succour the men on whose lives her life depended. The tradition of the "wise woman" still hung about her, and she had secret recipes for medicines that could cure almost any ill. When Aucassin fell from his horse and dislocated his shoulder, Nicolette set it for him. "She handled it so with her white hands and laboured so much that, by God's will who loves lovers, it came into its place; and then she took flowers and fresh grass and green leaves and bound them upon it with the flap of her chemise, and he was quite healed." In religion she learned the Pater Noster, the Ave and the Credo. She could read her book of hours and follow the mass.

The cult of the Virgin had virtually restored the feminine divinity of primitive religion, and men and women repeated daily the popular prayer to Mary which has been handed down in hundreds of manuscripts: "I come to-day to implore you, Virgin Mary. May you with all the saints and the elect of God be near me to give counsel and support for all my prayers and requests, in all my pains and necessities, in all that I am called upon to do, to say and to think, every day, every hour, every instant of my life."

It is necessary for our purpose to try to form a notion of what occupation the lady found for the greater number of the days, hours and instants of her life. The romantic vision that sees her dividing her time between awarding the prize at the tourney and presiding at the Court of Love may be abandoned at once. In its place there rises almost inevitably a picture somewhat nearer the truth, but drawn also from the romances and founded on the conditions of life at the courts of kings and great lords. There the simple structure of the castle had expanded, and with it the social structure. A great hall, separate from the donjon, was the theatre of stately action. Increased space brought with it a more complicated scheme of life. In the lord's castle were assembled for courtly education the sons and daughters of his vassals, who filled the place with gaiety. There was the frequent coming and going of guests, the solemn departure of the baron to war and his triumphant home-coming—the whole business, in a word, of the *chansons de geste* and the romances. We see the lady's life spent in perpetual summer-time. She spins with her maidens in the garden, while a comely youth recites a tale of love, or she wanders in the meadow gathering flowers for a chaplet. On the grass or in the hall she organises a merry dance of

damoisel with *damoiseau,* or she sits down to
play a game of chess with Sir Renaud, newly
returned from the Crusade. Even when her
good lord is gone to the Holy Land she enter-
tains freely and takes what cheer she may. It
is the *métier* of the romance to deal with•action,
and from it we receive inevitably the impression
of a stirring, animated life. Where the house
of the great lord is concerned this impression
may be measurably true, though even there we
must remember that winter came round at suitable intervals. But in the castle of the simple
knight, life, as far as we are able to reconstitute
it, must have passed with a monotony before
which the modern mind quails. When Gautier,
an enthusiast for the Middle Age, enumerates
the winter occupations of the castellan, he is
obliged to include sitting at the window and
watching the snow fall. The lady of the castle
was vigorous, and loved to be out of doors.
She rode, seated either astride or on what seems
to us the wrong side of the horse. She hunted
with the hawk and angled in the streams. She
was a strong walker and lover of animals, showing her love, as most animal lovers do, by petting
within doors and killing without. High physical courage was esteemed a virtue in her as in
her lord, for it is only in secure and peaceful
societies that the timid lady survives to transmit

her qualities. High physical courage should ideally beget tenderness for suffering, but the lady of the romances was sometimes a little inaccessible on the sympathetic side.

When William, Count of Orange, fled to his castle after his defeat by the paynim at Aliscans, with twenty thousand Turks in pursuit, he wore Saracen armour, and owed his life to the ruse. But Guibourc, his wife, did not recognise him, though she parleyed with him face to face, and would not open the gate. The good knight was the sole survivor of his army; he was wounded, and he had been fighting for sixty hours. But with one reproachful look at his hard-hearted lady, he turned upon the hundred Saracens who were immediately upon his heels and, single-handed, put them to flight and released their Christian captives. Then turning to Guibourc, who stood watching upon the gate, "Am I William?" he asked. This somewhat grotesque episode is founded on a real characteristic of the lady of the castle. As her knight fought for her honour she preferred him to incur danger rather than defeat; wounds and broken bones were, so to speak, all in the day's work. And when the day was won she succoured him tenderly.

The hardihood which served her well in crises was an invaluable element of daily life for herself and for her offspring, as it led her to healthy and vigorous out-of-door pastimes. But after the fullest allowance has been made for these pursuits, many empty hours remain unaccounted for. Life for the lady in the small castle must have had some similarity to life for women on the remote ranch to-day, if we eliminate the postal service and the library, and if we imagine that the ranchman is away from home as often as he can manage it, rounding up wild cattle, fighting Indians, trailing horse-thieves, or otherwise pleasurably endangering his life. His wife will probably learn to ride and shoot; she will busy herself with house-keeping, with her children or with her garden. But, after all, she can always read. The news-papers and the magazines find her out. She will keep herself supplied with books. And if the worst comes to the worst she will write a novel. The aspect of life that comes to the modern woman under the guise of literature had a different expression, though largely literary too, in the existence of the lonely châtelaine. In her case it came to be a reflection of the social development for which the age is noted, a spe-cific and original contribution to the history of the lady—I mean, of course, the theory and practice of courteous love. In looking closely at this institution it must be borne in mind that in the age of chivalry the wedded relation was not a romantic one. The husband was allowed by law to beat his wife for certain offences, and it is likely that he did not always wait to consult the code. The law, it is true, specified that he was to beat her "reasonably," and insisted that he must stop short of maiming her; he must not, for instance, destroy an eye or break a bone. Her marriage had been contracted without any necessary reference to inclination, and her relations with her husband were simply such as she was personally able to make them. With him her sole source of strength was her power to please, and that was naturally, as always, largely a matter of accident. He was under no manner of compulsion to try to please her. The fact, however, that she was his wife gave her importance with the rest of the world in proportion to his own, and from the standing-ground of this external importance she applied her lever to society.

In her lord's absence she commanded the castle; in his presence she shared the respect paid him by his subordinates. And the whole ordinary population of the castle consisted of subordinates. Not only his servants and men-at-arms, but the knights who held of him in fee and the squires who waited on him for military education observed towards him the etiquette of inferior to superior. This etiquette was strictly personal to him, and his wife had logically no right to share in it; but it was inevitably reflected on her by the sentiment that to-day makes the enlisted man in a lonely army post feel that the colonel's wife very nearly holds a commission herself. Like the colonel's wife, the knight's lady was the social head of the garrison; but she had the advantage of being free from competition with the wives of subalterns. If the visiting knight or squire had a wife, she stayed at home. The lady of the castle was virtually the only woman in a society consisting of men generally younger than herself who were socially her husband's inferiors, and who therefore paid court to her. If she had any personal force or charm these circumstances were highly favourable to its exertion. With her husband's importance her sphere of influence would vary from a single squire to a whole train of knights-vassal, but her position would tend to stereotype itself; so that the success of a great baron's wife in modifying the manners and the ideas of her husband's court would work to the advantage of the lonely châtelaine in the simple donjon. From the great centres would spread a theory of the lady's position and of the duty to her of every gentleman not her husband. Such a theory was developed and perfected in the twelfth and thirteenth centuries, and came by degrees to colour the whole of literature. The brutality of the old romances faded out, and an extraordinary code of manners came into fashion, based on a new theory of feminism and largely due to the initiative of influential women themselves. How far this theory actually modified life we are not in a position to say. It is certain, however, that every lady who listened to troubadour or jongleur, or who read for herself the new love-songs and romances, was furnished with the material for constructing a fresh estimate of her own importance. As Maître Jean Petit remarked in the thirteenth century: *En femme à puissance et vertu de faire de sen baron ou de sen ami le plus de sa volenté.*

II

IT is characteristic of the Middle Age to present us with an astonishing homogeneity of impression. One *chanson* is very like another, and the songs of the troubadours are in many cases interchangeable. Everything is done according to rule, with the striking combination, paradoxical, but found everywhere in primitive life and art, of the naïve and the conventional. Theology, war, law, art and education were elaborated into systems and welded upon society, which to this day shows the malformations due to their long pressure. In such an age it was not to be hoped that manners and the human heart could be left without a code after their existence had once been noticed. It is at the Court of Henry the First of England that scholars find the first development of "courtesy." This prince anticipated Fontainebleau and Versailles by the fêtes he arranged at his castles and the attention he gave to the organisation of bi-sexual society. Geoffrey of Monmouth, writing at the end of this reign a description of the ideal court of King Arthur, doubtless describes what he saw about him, a society (he says) which surpassed all others in luxury and in politeness, where knights were famous for prowess and ladies for courtesy, where the valour of knights encouraged the ladies to strive for womanly perfection, and the love of ladies spurred the valour of knights. If we may believe that the theory of courtesy, formulated in England, spread from this source into France, it is certain that it there encountered an independent development, sprung from the south, less warlike and more feminine in form, which was destined to prevail and give tone to the whole movement, not only in France, north and south, but throughout Europe.

South of the Loire the Roman law had always maintained a thread of continuity, though often obscured by usages springing directly from altered ways of living. By the Theodosian code, sons and daughters alike shared the inheritance of their father's estate, and this rule was taken over by the Gothic law of Southern France. But under the strain of the centuries that kept society perpetually on a war footing, the tendency prevailed even here to hold lands and houses in the strong hand. For her own safety the daughter was subordinated to the son. When the Saracens were finally disposed of a time of comparative quiet produced some very surprising results. That great material prosperity should follow was not surprising. The rich land blossomed like the rose; its vineyards not only made glad the heart of man but filled his purse; commerce developed and civic society began to feel assured of its existence; law was able to hold its own against might, and therefore the lady who was lawful owner of lands could hold them in peace. Many are the beautiful names of ladies who ruled in their own persons—Adelaide Countess of Carcassonne, Ermengarde Viscountess of Béziers,

Guillemette Viscountess of Nîmes, and the great Eleanor of Poitou, granddaughter of the first of the troubadours, Queen first of France and then of England, and always in her own right Duchess of Aquitaine. These ladies were almost by accident furnished with great power by a system devised for a society of a different character altogether. It is interesting to consider the amazement with which Theodosius would have viewed the career of Ermengarde Viscountess of Narbonne, who, although twice married, ruled her principality with her own hand for sixty years and fought her own battles with success. As in the case of the lady abbess, feudalism played into the hands of the very persons to whose interests it was apparently inimical. A form of society devised and carried on by men became suddenly a source of strength to women. And the most surprising thing of all is that the women in whose hands power was thus placed proved to be able to use it. Instead of showing as the atrophied remnant of a suppressed class, ready to govern in name but in reality to be governed by the nearest man, and to carry on a society and a culture imitative of that erected by men everywhere about them, they proved to be themselves personages capable of forming reasoned designs and making them prevail, and they effected changes in society and culture that have become a permanent part of the life of Europe.

It has often been pointed out that there are certain analogies between the period of the Crusades and the nineteenth century in the United States in respect of the distribution of culture between the sexes. In Greece and in Rome of old, as in Germany in the last century, and in general at times and in places where men have leisure for culture, it is believed to belong more or less exclusively to the male type. It is felt at such times to be unsuitable for women. The learned or the thoughtful woman is rather ridiculous, and certainly a bore. Probably she neglects her children. On the other hand, when men are as a class engaged in the subjugation of the natural world or in struggles with each other, the arts of peace naturally fall into the hands of non-combatants, and are then believed to belong more or less exclusively to the female type. As under the other conditions culture is felt to be unbecoming in woman, it is now felt to be unbecoming in man. A fighting knight who found his squire reading the *Ars Amatoria* would feel the same amused contempt as a stockbroker who should find his clerk secreting a copy of Keats behind the ticker. To the mind of each such interests would be suitable only

to women and to certain men—"priests" the
crusader would have called them, "college pro-
fessors" the broker. In both periods the lady
has been the depository and guardian of
culture. What she has made of her position in
modern times must be discussed elsewhere.
Her achievements in the twelfth and thirteenth
centuries are matter of record, and we must
now examine them.

It is obvious that the automatic result of making a lady the head of the state will be to furnish
her court with persons whose recommendations
to favour will differ from those offered to a
male superior. It will, of course, be to her interest to employ and attach to herself a body of
strong fighting men, but she will not be interested in personally observing their readiness
for combat and their power to drink without
drunkenness. To be pleasant to his lady a
servant must develop other gifts. In the technical language of the time, courtesy must
accompany prowess. | Grafted upon the funda-
mental point of view of the fighting knight, and
in many respects opposed to it, was a secondary
set of ideas which, by the transforming power
of literature, has become to us the strongest
element of the whole. By chivalry we mean
to-day not the strong, hard framework of military society which prevailed for centuries in

Europe, unregardful of women if not cruel to them, but we mean the brief and local phase, confined chiefly to the great courts, which, by passing into literature, has forever clothed the knight with virtues and sentiments not (if all had their rights) his own." The constraint that was put upon the man who looked for preferment in a lady's service to be clean and civil, pleasant to look at and pleasant to hear, and an ardent advocate of the intellectual and moral supremacy of women, was but a small and ephemeral result of her power. The real result was attained when the men of genius had constructed and won acceptance everywhere for a whole theory of life based on the superiority of the lady. At all times, everywhere and by all ladies, love is admitted to be the most acceptable of gifts. With tact the humblest may offer it without offence, the highest without conferring obligation. The lady's power to excite love was to her what the lord's prowess in battle was to him. The new theory of life was therefore based upon a new theory of love, and into this new theory were worked up a number of old elements that would have seemed singly rather unpromising material.

One of the fundamental principles of the doctrine of courteous love was its incompatibility with marriage. It is true that no age of men had imagined that love and marriage were ever, except by accident, coincident. Since marriage is primarily founded on economic considerations, the continued effort of mankind to make its sentimental aspect prevail involves a paradox. The Athenians, as we have seen, looked not to their wives for love's delight. The Romans were not authorities on love, but what they knew by that name was not a domestic sentiment. Early Christianity also considered marriage as a duty rather than a pleasure. But these different societies had felt the irksomeness of the bond from the man's point of view; it was in conflict with one of the characteristics that had been most serviceable in helping him along in the world—his unquenchable desire of novelty. Courtesy, on the other hand, objected to marriage from the point of view of the wife. Courtesy maintained that a lady's love should be free. The mere fact that in marriage she was bound by law to yield her favours destroyed their value and her dignity. Even if she married her lover, she thereby extinguished love. *Amour de grace* and *amour de dette* were discriminated by the doctors, who held the first only to be worthy of the name of love. No true lover would accept love save as a gift of free will. The lady might withhold her favour with reason or without; treason to love consisted in bestowing it for any reason save love alone. But it was not as a pretext for frequent change that the lady exalted love at the expense of marriage. On the contrary, it behoved her to choose her lover with far greater care than her husband (says Sordello in his *Ensenhamen d'Onor*), because love is *plus fort establit*. Husband and wife may be parted by divers accidents, *mas no es res que puesc' amors, ses mort, partir*. If we were to represent the history of marriage graphically by a straight line, and the history of love by a curve approaching marriage more or less closely, we should find the lady's theory of love soaring as far above marriage toward the ideal as Ovid's theory falls below it toward the beast. His criticism of marriage was that it was too good; hers that it was not good enough. The striking modernism of this view is more apparent than real. The lady dreamed of no reconstruction of society; marriage was her portion, and she accepted it. Love did not interfere with it—did not, in fact, lie in the same plane. Her criticism of marriage was suggested and enforced by a number of circumstances besides her own personal revolt from it. The poets who embodied her ideas were generally of a class below her own, and under chivalry there was no marriage possible between classes. The singer who offered homage to his lady must find some footing on which he could address her without too servile an acknowledgment of inferiority. Nothing could have served his purpose so well as the theory that love is the great leveller, but that every lover is his lady's servant. Besides the barriers to marriage erected by feudal society, the Cluniac reform was insisting on the celibacy of the clergy, but many a troubadour was either monk or priest. For him also it was valuable that love should keep clear of marriage.

The old May songs celebrating spring-time and the naïve mating impulse had come down without a break from immemorial heathendom, from the dim time when mating was coterminous with desire. And these May songs, with the necessary transformations, were taken up into the song of the troubadour. With their eternal cry of spring they are, indeed, wherever they leave their trace, in epic or conte or song, almost the only note of Nature in the literature of the Middle Age. The nightingale, the budding flowers, the clear skies of spring, are all that the knight notices of the world's aspect. Their imagery becomes greasy with handling as singer after singer compares the birth of love with the birth of summer. Charmed at first with what he has taken to be evidence of the poet's communion with Nature, the reader is soon driven to recognise a pure convention. The natural world has little to say to the troubadour. His world is within, and if he had not needed the eroticism of the May song he would have given scant heed to the nightingale. From the May song he drew the "joy" that gave a name to his science and a crude literal view of the delight of love. But the joy came gradually to have a more spiritual content. What the lady demanded was to be loved for her soul. As the type reached perfection the May song element dissolved into the mysticism that was to culminate in Dante's love for Beatrice.

III

THE tendency of the Middle Age toward the neat, the systematic and the en- cyclopædic, which made it so easy a prey to Aristotle, had the oddest results when directed toward the passion of love. Ovid's *jeu d'esprit,* the *Ars Amatoria,* was playfully set in a framework of Alexandrian didacticism. It was mildly amusing in his day to assume that rules could be laid down by the use of which anyone could become "a master of the art of love," to use the phrase of Diotima in Plato's *Symposium*. This work was well-known to clerks in its Latin form, and when love became a matter of general theoretical interest it was rendered into French, and became the text-book of the subject. Thanks to its method, love became a department of scholasticism, a matter of definition and rule. In the complete absence of the historic sense, which left the mediæval mind with no more perspective than the paintings on a castle wall, Ovid's badinage became matter for debate. The social conditions assumed in every line of his work were unnoticed. He wrote of and for the sophisticated dwellers in a great town, for the members of a cosmopolitan society whose intercourse was unrestrained, for a cultivated public well used to literary allusion and to the appreciation of the half-word—for life, in a word, as we know it to-day and as the Romans knew it two thousand years ago. But the knight and the lady of the castle knew no such life. Their days were spent in a simple round among a small number of people, all ignorant and all literal-minded. Their irruptions into the world, whether for war or for gaiety, were infrequent and for specific purposes. They were utterly without the daily contact with many minds, which was the postulate of Ovid's psychology. As Gaston Paris remarks: "To tell the truth, the Middle Age, with its profound incapacity to form a picture of anything but itself, was never aware of the abyss that lay between it and the ancient world. It peacefully translated *miles* by *cavalier,* or *pontifex* by *bishop,* without dreaming of the difference between the ideas represented by these words." It is touching to see the steps by which, under these conditions, the doctors of courteous love proceeded to Christianise and feudalise their great Latin authority. When Ovid advises the enterprising young man to frequent the theatres whither the ladies go, both to see the show and show themselves, Maître Elies can find no modern parallel but the churches. Thither the ladies all go, some to pray to God, but the greater number to see and to be seen. Ovid suggests to the Roman to seat himself at the circus close to the lady he wishes to charm and give her tips on the horses. Maître Elies sends his pupil to a miracle play, and bids him ask the lady questions about the cast: "Which are laymen? Who is that old man? Who is he in the furred cloak?" In general the early versions of Ovid are more decent than the original; when they are gross the Roman's refinement of vice is not reproduced. In some cases the imitator ventures to differ from the original. Thus the author of the *Key to Love* says: "Ovid will have us believe that it is better to have an old woman for one's love than a young one, but with all respect I cannot agree with him. Ovid, I imagine, needed money; what he feels is avarice, not love. The love that joins gentle hearts goes straight on its way without simony." The whole process by which a theology of love grew up, nourished by the thoughts and language of the church, is foreshadowed by this unknown clerk, to whom venal love is "simony." Some items of advice are put into the Roman author's mouth that would have surprised him: for instance, "Be sure there are no wrinkles in your stockings; this is Ovid's express command."

When Eleanor of Aquitaine, her daughter Marie of Champagne, and the other *précieuses* had arrived through much discussion at a fairly clear idea of what they wanted, the work of compiling their canon law was confided to the author of the *Art of Honourable Love,* probably Andreas Capellanus, who was at once the Gerson and the Aquinas of the passion. No more amusing game was ever invented for the entertainment of polite society than the methodical discussion of love. It contained something for everyone. Under cover of its high moral pretensions and scientific aims anything could be said. The earnest and the frivolous, the amorous and the cool, the devout and the careless, all were furnished with a decorous means of approach to the most fascinating topic in the world. Two standards are visible in the chaplain's work—the first, shorter and more famous code of law embodies a higher ideal of the subject in hand than the longer one. Concessions are made to the natural man. But, on the whole, Ovid's metamorphosis is complete. Where he enjoined the giving of gifts as a means of vulgar seduction, courtesy held that the present was a tribute from vassal to suzerain. Ovid recommends secrecy to the lover for self-preservation, but the code commands it for the lady's sake. Ovid realised that leanness and pallor are convenient to a lover, who should assume them if he have them not, to work upon the feelings of his mistress. In her presence he should tremble and grow pale. According to the chaplain, one of the signs of a true lover is his physical disturbance in presence of the beloved. It is an axiom of the science that the sudden sight of the lady alters the lover's circulation. The words are the words of Ovid, and the emotion is not just that of Sappho. Nevertheless, if a little goodwill went to produce the vaso-motor disturbance that was the sign of love, it was applied with the intent not to deceive the lady, but to play the game. The spirit of the code can be gathered from a few examples:—

1. Marriage is not a valid excuse from love.

13. Common love seldom endures.

15. Every lover is wont to grow pale at sight of the beloved.

18. Virtue alone makes one worthy of love.

23. The thought of love makes a man sleep less and eat less.

24. Every action of the lover ends in thoughts of the beloved.

25. The true lover cares for nothing save what he deems pleasant to the beloved.

30. The true lover is forever and without interruption occupied by the image of the beloved.

Among the theses often debated by the learned in love were those that dealt with the relative desirability of a knight or a clerk as a lover, and as the clerks controlled the records, they have, as far as literature goes, the best of it. The *Council of Remiremont,* a Latin poem of probably the twelfth or thirteenth century, gives us a fanciful account of a debate on this topic, set in a framework of light-hearted blasphemy. A group of religious ladies, presided over by a "lady cardinal," meet (of course, in spring-time) behind closed doors, expelling all men save a few honest clerks, and all women past the age of joy. Beginning with a parody on the office of the church, one of the company reads for gospel a passage from Ovid, and two others sing hymns of love. There follows a spirited debate between the advocates of clerks and those of knights. The clerks have the best of it; the sense of the meeting is that it is good to choose them as lovers, for "their love is a great delight." An order of excommunication against rebels is drawn up in the name of Venus: "To you and others everywhere who yield to the love of knights let there remain confusion, terror, contrition and many other curses. Amen."

The debate was one of the most congenial exercises of the Middle Age. To defend a thesis was in some sort to ride a tilt. During the long centuries when the church was occupied with the *chimæra bombinans in vacuo,* society dealt with questions of greater interest. A lady grieves for a lover taken in battle; a squire cannot cease to love a lady who despises him. Which is the more worthy of pity? A fair lady, deserted by her first love, bestows her affections on a second; is she perjured? Of these four ladies, which is the most pitiable—she whose lover was slain in battle; she whose lover was taken prisoner; she whose lover has not been heard of since the battle; she whose lover ran away? Which lady is more lovable—the foolish beauty or the plain-featured wit? Are men or women the more constant in love?

The actual songs themselves of the troubadours and minnesingers, oddest of love lyrics, are full of the spirit of scholasticism. Instead of the personal cry they give an argument on the general case. Absorbed in a technical discussion of the nature of love, the poet sometimes forgot altogether to explain his personal interest in the subject. The traditionalism of theology was strong in him. The progress of his art was in form alone; like the theologian, he was content to work over and over an established body of material. Like the theologian, he combined by main strength the most disparate elements, not noticing their essential antagonism if he could bring about a formal union. In many a song he lectured to his beloved on the psychology and ethics of their common experience. From the body he had worked his way up to the mind; before the movement was spent and the Middle Age disintegrated he had reached the soul.

The prevalence of formal discussion, the immense allegorical literature of the Courts of

Love, and certain notices of the decisions of great ladies, made arbiters in real cases, gave rise at one time to the notion that the court of love was an actual institution whose action was binding on lovers in its jurisdiction. It is generally admitted to-day, however, that the evidence never supported such a theory, and that therefore its intrinsic improbability is conclusive against it. Secrecy in love was among the lover's first duties. Loyalty, secrecy and diligence are often given as his cardinal virtues. *Estre secret et plaisant* was his formula. It is manifestly absurd to suppose that a sentiment which depended on concealment for its existence should be amenable to public inquiry. Doubtless many a case, theoretically a secret, was dealt with by innuendo; and doubtless many an abstract decision delivered by a great lady was felt to have a definite address. But the idea that the courteous relation was capable of being haled before an actual court needs only to be stated to be abandoned.

IV

THE professional troubadour might be attached to a court for a short time only, and without payment of any kind. The prizes of life consisted for him in permanent awards of land or office, and later of money. The commonest fate was half way between these situations; he lived at court as an enlivener of society, and was furnished with bed and board, and in favourable cases with arms and clothing. The songs are full of prayers for the opportunity of service and for the substantial reward of service. The pretty language of feudal relations, easily sliding into allegory even then, gives romance to-day to the singer's cry. Not only to ladies, but to lords, he offers true and loyal service. Walther von der Vogelweide advertises that he is ready to serve any gentleman or lady who will reward him. Often a poet recommends himself in impassioned language to a lady whom he has never seen. On the other hand, he frequently reminds her that he has been her servant from his childhood. It is interesting to ask oneself how far this claim, so often urged, doubtless less truthfully in some cases than in others, becoming part of the technique of the genre, determined the fact that Dante's passion dated from his tenth year. The troubadour generally vowed that his service should last as long as his life; yet he often changed his allegiance, and sometimes set off his praise of the new mistress by disparagement of the old. According to the formula, occurring again and again in song and romance, the singer's duty was twofold—to serve and to honour. The poetic fiction of a love relation was inevitably suggested by the ordinary language of feudal devotion. The deep gulf that separated vassal from lady might be crossed by the cry of a hopeless and respectful love. Very often the lady is reproached for her pride; she will not so much as cast the glance that will save her servant from death. Of course, the reproach is really flattery; it means, in fact, that the lady is above reproach. The usages of feudalism lent themselves excellently to erotic purposes. The vassal kneels before his lord, lays his folded hands in those of his lord, kisses his feet, and is kissed by him on the mouth. In the epics the kiss is often momentous. In the *Four Sons of Aymon,* to give a single example, King Eudo kisses his vassal Renaut on receiving him; afterwards, having privily betrayed him, he dismisses him without the kiss, feigning illness to excuse the omission. It is true that the troubadour's kiss had a double parentage, being descended on one side from Ovid and the May song; but the true kiss of courtesy was the sacramental and mystic sign of love's devout allegiance. An axiom of feudalism declared, "The higher the lord the better the vassal." In accordance with this principle the troubadour was able to celebrate his mistress's worldly station and its reflection on himself. There was nothing in the relation of servant and mistress to prevent a lady from retaining several singers at once. It is somewhat more singular that the singer was able to consecrate his genius to more than one lady at a time. He accomplished this logically by saying to each that her virtues ennobled her whole sex, so that all ladies were revered by him.

It has been the conviction of certain critics that the minnesong was the pæan of lawless love. There can be no doubt that where lawless love existed the conventions of courtesy and the minnesong fitted its exigencies to perfection, and we shall consider it later in connection with the romances of Chrétien de Troyes. But the love of the professional troubadour was official. His business was to glorify his lady. It was his song that she wanted and rewarded, not his passion. Personally, he was probably of no great importance to her. This is what he means by saying that timidity prevents him from declaring his love otherwise than in song. This is true even of the non-professional troubadour. The great lords who sang to ladies used humble language, and offered the most extreme devotion as a delicate attention. Often the singer felt obliged to assure the world that his lady was cruel and his wishes unfulfilled. Particularly in Germany, where manners were strict, the poet took care not to be misunderstood. Only thus can we explain the fact that a literature by definition "gay," explicitly devised for the entertainment of a light-hearted society, should be filled with the pain of disappointed love. The troubadour's usual state of mind is desire. He often declares that he would rather love his mistress in vain than win another woman. Often he speaks of his love as an illusion:

"Ich diene immer auf den minnelichen Wahn."

The ladies of all singers are alike; their beauty is described by formula; out of thousands of songs not one lady can be identified as a person; there is a typical lady, but there are no individuals. Every singer makes the same protestations and complaints. It is his rhymes that he is thinking of. Every singer declares that all the others are making believe; he alone is serious. There are many traces of jealousy of the amateur, the lordly troubadour who may approach the lady in daily life, thus gaining a great advantage over his lowly competitor, and who sings for nothing. Generally the lady is named or identified. When a feigned name is used it has the air of being as well known as the real one. It is unthinkable that a favoured lover should thus compromise a great lady. Sometimes a song was addressed to a lady and her husband, to a lady and her brother, to a lady and her nephews! It is not maintained that the troubadour never felt love, nor is it likely that he could constantly handle fire without a scorch. But it is very likely that too sincere a feeling was disadvantageous to him. Bernard of Ventadorn, the most impassioned of the school, has frequent occasion to sing a song of parting. Perhaps the most fortunate case for a troubadour was that he should love, for the sake of the effect on his talent, but that his beloved should not be the lady to whom his songs were addressed. The *précieuse* did not wish to command the whirlwind. *Mezura* (moderation) was one of the qualities required of the courteous lover.

V

IF minnesong had consisted simply of the elements we have considered, the crude sensualism of the May song, the gallantry of Ovid and the compliments of a court singer, it would not have survived to have a lasting effect on the literature of Europe. But a man did not live in the eleventh century or the twelfth for nothing; whether he were clerk or layman he submitted to the feeling of the time that the "eye of the heart" could see realities that the bodily eye would never find. St. Bernard and Bernard of Ventadorn were at one on this point. The thirtieth rule of Andreas Capellanus rested on it. The beautiful word *minne* itself illustrates the history of the idea. The earliest singers of Germany do not use it; *friuntschaft* and *liebe* are their words for love. The root-meaning of *minnen* is *to think of.* Its gradual prevalence accompanies the transfer of sexual love into the spiritual life. The love of a lady whom the lover has never seen occurs in romantic literature everywhere, from the *Arabian Nights* to the *Nibelungen Lied.* In courteous love it became classic.

The beautiful legend of Jaufre Rudel, created to explain his famous songs of love from afar, and used by Rostand in his *Princesse Lointaine,* bespeaks its importance: "Now Jaufre Rudel of Blaia was a right noble prince of Blaia, and it chanced that, though he had not seen, he loved the Countess of Tripoli for her great excellence and virtue, whereof the pilgrims who came from Antioch spread abroad the report. And he made of her fair songs with fair melodies and with short verses, till he longed so greatly to see her that he took the Cross and embarked upon the sea to gain sight of her. And lo! in the ship there fell upon him such great sickness that they who were with him weened he was dead therein; nathless they brought him as one dead to a hostelry in Tripoli. And the thing was made known to the Countess, so that she came unto his bedside and took him into her arms. Then he knew that it was she, and sight and speech returned unto him, and he gave praise and thanks unto God who had preserved his life until his seeing her. And so he died in the arms of the Countess, and she gave him honourable burial in the temple-house of Tripoli; and on that selfsame day she gave herself to God and became a nun, for loss of him and grief at his death."

The dream was a glimpse of reality in the Middle Age. Monk or nun dreamed of salvation, often with an erotic tinge. Love in a dream was the lover's solace. The misery of

waking life was felt alike by saint and by lover.
The thought of death was familiar and not
unwelcome to both. Ovid had spoken in sheer
rhetoric of dying for love; the mediæval lover
was ready to die in earnest. The love of a dead
lady was often sung, with a cast forward to
Beatrice. Tears are an innovation of the
courteous lover. They are shed not at all in
Beowulf, but sparingly in the *Nibelungen
Lied,* and hardly oftener in the *chansons* and
early epics. But St. Bernard and the troubadour weep freely. The mystic, whether in love
or in religion, was subject to ecstasy. The
Lancelot of *Chrétien de Troyes* was twice in
great bodily peril because the sudden sight of his
lady bereft him of attention to the rest of his environment. The way is being prepared for
Dante's swoon at the marriage feast. In a
word, the mysticism of the troubadour, passing
into Italy and there modified, was adopted by
the *dolce stil nuovo* and reached its climax in
the work of the great poet of the Middle Age.

A very different history awaited it in the
north. At the court of Marie de Champagne,
impregnated with the ideas of courtesy, lived
Chrétien de Troyes, the father of the psychological romance. In his hands the laws of love
were worked out in their application to life.

Gaston Paris, in an essay of incomparable insight, has analysed the elements that go to the making of Chrétien's *Conte de la Charrette*. This romance tells how Guinevere, Arthur's queen, was carried away by Méléguant, a discourteous lover, and rescued by Lancelot. According to the analysis of Paris, the germ of the story is an ancient Breton legend of a king's wife, who was stolen by the king of the dead and recovered by her husband. In course of time the queen is specified as the wife of Arthur, and Arthur is her deliverer. At the same time, or soon after, the king of the dead loses his mythological character and becomes Maelwas, King of Somerset; but traces of his origin cling to him, for even in Chrétien's story it is said that from his country no traveller returns, and it is reached by marvellous means. At this stage the Breton story passed into Anglo-Norman poetry, and for Arthur was substituted Lancelot, who was, however, not yet the lover of Guinevere. Chrétien had before him this Anglo-Norman version. His contribution to the story, besides a number of adventurous complications of a somewhat commonplace character, presented for the first time in literature a complete picture of the knightly lover. In the earlier versions of Lancelot's story he delivered Guinevere merely in performance of his duty as a brave knight. Chrétien made him her lover, affecting by this stroke not only the fate of Paolo and Francesca, but the experience of the reading public from that day to this. Lancelot's life is dominated by his *idée fixe*. The love of other women is repugnant to him. No sacrifice is too great if made for his lady's sake. To save her he incurs every imaginable danger. This, however, is routine for any brave knight; the real trial comes when, in order to find her, he is obliged to ride for a distance on a cart, an act which, for reasons not explained, had something shameful in it. For a moment he hesitates to incur this shame, but then for love's sake accepts it. After all his adventures Guinevere receives him coldly, and the explanation embodies all the subtlety of the laws of love. Lancelot believes it was because he had mounted upon the cart and incurred shame. Not so; it was because for a moment he had hesitated to do so. He humbly acknowledges his fault, and the penance for this knight, the bravest of the brave, is to let himself appear a coward. His love is the motive of his life, and his lady is the judge of all his actions. When he is standing at a castle window overlooking the plain far below he sees his lady pass, and would throw himself down did not his companion restrain him. Finding on his toilsome road a comb with some of his lady's hairs in it, this strong man sinks nerveless to the ground. On her part the lady is equally ideal as an exemplar of the code. Her courtesy and grace are unfailingly exerted, on foe as on friend. She loves Lancelot as he loves her. When she thinks him dead she begins to starve herself. But in spite of her passion she never loses sight of her duty as a source of moral uplift to her lover. When he finally wins his way to her she receives him with severity, reproaching him with his instant of hesitation and fixing his heavy fine. But when this is paid he receives his full reward. Neither of the lovers has a moment of misgiving or remorse. Guinevere is Arthur's wife, and Lancelot is his sworn knight, but neither gives him a thought. As Andreas Capellanus described the theory of courteous love, so does Chrétien describe its practice. Its essence consists in standing outside of marriage. The lady's favour is revocable at any time, and the lover stands in perpetual fear of losing it. She governs him both by fear and by gratitude; by fear, since she is his not for life but for good behaviour; by gratitude, because for his sake she runs the terrible risk of her husband's anger.

The lady thus achieved for herself a very strong position. To be worthy of her the lover accomplished marvels of prowess, and she was preoccupied with his spiritual progress. Both

admitted that their love was an art, governed
by rules and precedents. She had freed herself from the limitations of marriage, but from
the noblest possible motives. The tabu was
broken in the interests of a higher morality.
The husband was placed among the Philistines
by the very conditions of his tenure; he could
find room among the finer spirits only by qual-
ifying as a lover and receiving from some other
woman the education his wife was dispensing
to another man. "Goodness is the only worthy
crown of love," said the official expositor.
Love as known to Ovid was a degradation; to
the troubadour it was a means of grace.
Courtesy could say with St. Augustine, *Faciunt
boni amores bonos mores.*

THE LADY OF THE RENAISSANCE

Et encore ai-je une opinion, dit Parlamente, que jamais homme n'aimera parfaitement Dieu, qu'il n'ait parfaitement aimé quelque créature en ce monde.—MARGARET, QUEEN OF NAVARRE: *The Heptameron.*

I

IN the frescoes with which Benozzo Gozzoli in the fifteenth century adorned the walls of the Campo Santo in Pisa and of the church of San Gimignano, there are preserved for us the portraits of a type of house which survives nowhere except in these paintings, and which marks a great social change. We can trust Gozzoli's accuracy. The artists of his day were students of all the constructive arts, and as ready to build a bridge as to paint a Madonna. Their backgrounds sometimes portray a whole city, worked out with the care of an architect's plan. Wherever we are able to check Gozzoli, we find that he tells the literal truth about the appearance of the world of his day, and we can therefore safely make, on his authority, certain statements about the dwellings of the well-to-do in Italy in his century.

The traditions of Roman architecture had never been altogether drowned out in Italy by the Gothic; and the discovery at the end of the thirteenth century of the manuscript of Vitruvius, the great Roman architect, renewed the authority of these traditions. The Gothic ideas were soon abandoned and left their mark only in the shape of a certain eclecticism and liberty of fancy which prevented the slavish reproduction of the antique. For although the houses of Gozzoli are far nearer to the Roman villa than to the Gothic donjon, they have nevertheless a radical difference. The Roman house, like the Greek house, presented as nearly as possible a blank wall to the world. Within there was space, air and light, but no one could guess it from without. The early Italian house on the other hand is open and accessible. The people who live in it wish to see and are willing to be seen. Contrasting the house with the donjon we can see that life has become relatively safe and peaceful; contrasting it with the Roman house we can see that life has become democratic and simple. In a word, it has become modern. The loggia has appeared with all its social connotation. It may occur on the ground floor, on the first floor or on the roof; it may be covered with trellised vines or with a roof, and sometimes another story rests upon it. The balcony is there with no roof at all. The roof of the house is covered with tiles or lead and serves as a terrace. Sometimes vines and shrubs are planted there. The houses are entered by gracious porticos, inviting the guest instead of forbidding him. Doors and windows open freely on the ground floor as on all the others. In one instance the main entrance of a modest little house is guarded by a curtain only. The charming verandah on which the good Gozzoli has displayed the drunkenness of Noah has many of the characteristics of the democratised classical forms that we Americans call "colonial." These dignified yet highly ornamented exteriors lend themselves readily to the requirements of popular and civic gaiety; carpets and draperies and garlands fall naturally into their lines. The spirit of them was not confined to the luxurious house of the wealthy citizen, but entered into the palaces of the Renaissance in Italy. In France the day of the donjon passed. Either the castellan added extraneous buildings in which everyday life was carried on, retaining the keep for emergencies only; or he abandoned the keep altogether and built for himself the beautiful Renaissance château with a semblance of fortification but primarily a house to live in. Visitors to Chenonceaux remember the isolated tower standing at the left of the château and a little in advance of it. This is the surviving donjon of Pierre de Marques, ancient lord of the manor. But door, gable and windows were added by Thomas Bohier, Baron de Saint Ciergue, who acquired the property under Francis the First. Bohier's building is living proof that the function of a man's house was changed; it was no longer constructed primarily for the repulse of his enemies but for the reception of his friends. The donjon has become positively gay in appearance, and it gives an object-lesson of the ingenuity employed in supplying it with what it chiefly lacked as a human habitation—windows, namely—without weakening the walls. The architect boldly cut out a section of the solid masonry from top to bottom, and replaced it with pilastered windows, strongly mullioned, the upper supported by the lower. Nothing could be more charming in effect. The donjon proverbially frowns, but that of Chenonceaux is made to smile. The main body of the château, built from the beginning by Bohier, preserves, to save its face, some signs of the Gothic and military origin of its type; but the turrets have lost their machicolation, a very modern improvement in its day to facilitate the pouring of molten lead on the heads of besiegers. A peaceful cornice has taken its place. The *salle d'armes* has become a drawing-room; the lady has a boudoir; the loop-hole has become the most beautiful of windows; and the dark and difficult staircase has become a stately construction.

The Italian palace made haste to profit by times of peace, and even to take chances in time of war, by venturing out from the city-walls and becoming a villa. So thoroughly was the open air recognised as the first luxury of life, that the garden was regarded as an integral part of the house. And if the house was Roman, far more so was the garden. Climate naturally had here a determining voice. In relation to his garden the fifteenth century Italian had much more in common with the ancient Roman than with the Englishman or even the Frenchman of his own day. In Italy the difference between indoors and out is conventional, in more northern countries it is essential. The Frenchman and the Englishman learned in time to consider house and garden in relation to each other but they never lost sight of the fact that they are different things. In Italy the infrequence of the chimney withindoors and the conformation of the garden without tell the same story of the kindliness of nature. The builder of the Renaissance therefore planned his garden as nearly as possible in the spirit in which the imperial Roman had planned his. Neither of them approached it in the spirit of the Englishman who aims at an imitation of nature. With the somewhat hard logic characteristic of the æsthetic of both, the imperial Roman and the Italian of the Renaissance agreed that nature cannot be imitated. She can however be subdued and made amenable to art, for which her tissues and processes make one of the most beautiful of mediums. It is not necessary to describe here the varied beauties of the Italian villa, or to recall its effects on the ideas and practices of other lands. Its charming forms will recur of themselves to anyone who has seen the Villa Madama, the Villa d'Este, the Villa Lante, the Villa Aldobrandini. Their intrinsic beauty is not our theme, but their bearing on the status of the lady. Their general social import has already been hinted; their very existence implied an established order, a leisure class, the opportunity and the will to make the most of life. It is when such conditions prevail that the lady blooms. In time of stress she is classed with the impedimenta. When men are in the saddle, their women are put away with the other treasures and household gear, to be fought for to the death but hardly to be enjoyed or displayed to admiring friends. But if the lady had acquired some dust and cobwebs during the fighting times of the middle age, her period of renovation was at hand. Not only had the men of the Renaissance time to get out their works of art, but they had the taste for them. They might quite easily, as far as one can see, have taken to commerce or to drink, but as a matter of fact they took to visible beauty. The lady became indispensable for her decorative value. She was treated, it is true, very much as inanimate nature was treated; that is, she was transformed into a work of art. She had her inevitable place in the pageant of life, as in some splendid arrangement of society by Veronese. Her limits were set not so much by economic conditions or by the egotism of man as by the collective æsthetic sense. We may say that in the general collapse of institutionalism and authority which astonished the fifteenth century, the only positive demand made of the lady was that she should be beautiful. This might seem at first sight the harshest of all demands, but it should be added at once that to the almost superhumanly intelligent eye of that age there were very nearly as many ways of being beautiful as there were ladies. Oddly enough it is the periods without an eye, like our own, and the periods when the eye is subject to limitations, like the middle age, that are difficult in the matter of the lady's appearance. At such times there are only two or three ways of being beautiful, and to one of these the lady must conform or be missed altogether. Like any other object of art she must belong to an easily recognised group; and this principle the dealers understand very well, turning out the required article with amazing uniformity, so that a word from Burne-Jones or Mr. Gibson determines the physical characters of many seasons of débutantes. The great gift of the men of the Renaissance, inexplicable and paid for by limitations in some other directions, was an unusually widely diffused power to judge of visible beauty. At first thought we might feel that the great collector of the Renaissance was the same person as the great collector of our own day. A second thought reveals the gulf between them. The Renaissance collector used his own judgment, and it was based on the æsthetic merit of the object. The collector of our day uses in general the judgment of some one else,—of some individual or of society at large. And if he does choose for himself, his choice is based on the same shrewd commercial instinct for a "good thing" which, employed in other fields, is the cause of his being in a position to buy objects of art at all. Collectors of this sort are generally most interested in the old, for it requires a different equipment to judge the new. The Renaissance could not, it is true, get enough of the old, but no age since that of the Greeks has so intrepidly encouraged the new. This freedom of judgment was favourable to the lady, who generally remains a dogma even in ages that have surrendered all others.

If the collector was propitious to the lady in his appreciation and anxious to make the most of her, the artist was also, as he always is, her natural ally. The feminine strand often recognised in the artist's psychology seems to be the natural result of the fact that he alone of men has some share in the determining experience of a woman's life,—maternity. His nerves like hers are played upon by the long unintermittent drain of gestation and by the bitter-sweet anguish of production. He knows what it is to feel his vitality, his will-power, the very food he eats, go to the benefit of something not himself, something to which he is sacrificed. His famous temperament represents his vague consciousness of how important it is to society that all should go well with him. And when the child or the work of art is finally born, the father and the collector, for all their enthusiasm, are in one class; the artist and the mother are in another, for they agree in valuing

the product not only for what it is worth, or
from a sense of proprietorship, but for what it
has cost.

Like the tree in the garden, the lady had often
to undergo a certain amount of modification
before she was felt to be in harmony with the
rest of the composition. Two direct inherit-
ances from imperial Rome were the art of the
topiarius, who could make a shrub into a pea-
cock, and the transformation of the darkest
hair to golden red. The famous recipe of the
Countess Nani, to produce the shade called
filo d'oro, required two pounds of alum, six
ounces of black sulphur and four ounces of
honey, the whole to be diluted with water.
Titian's cousin, Cesare Vecellio, tells us how
the preparation was applied. The lady, having
thoroughly anointed her hair, established herself on some retired terrace open to the sun, and
set upon her head the brim of a great hat with
no crown. Through the central opening she
drew her hair and spread it on the expansive
brim, thus exposing her locks to the sunlight and
at the same time preserving her complexion.
For hours she sat and sunned herself until the
lotion was dry and the colour fixed, patiently
preparing herself to become a congenial subject
for Titian's pallette.

In the course of the Renaissance the lady

developed a waist. In the middle age her garments had been all of a piece, sometimes girdled more or less closely, but characterised by long lines from shoulder to toe. Her lamentable modern conception of herself as consisting of two parts, an upper and a lower, susceptible of different architectural treatment, dates most unexpectedly from an age of beauty. Gentile Bellini's kneeling Venetian lady (blonde of course) has cut off her tight-fitting bodice at the waist and sewn her skirt to it. Bernardo Zenale's equally blonde lady has done the same thing. The next step was to make bodice and skirt of different colours, and the lady was sawn asunder, with as happy effect as if a Doric column were to be painted two-thirds red and one-third yellow.

The mechanical difficulty of adjusting a tight bodice to the curves of the human body was met at an early date by the application down the middle line in front of a strip of some unyielding substance. This object was often exposed to view, when it was made of ivory or silver or mother-of-pearl, and richly ornamented. Sometimes it bore a charming inscription. On one that was worn by Anne of Austria is engraved a posy beginning thus: *"Ma place ordinairement est sur le coeur de ma maitresse."* Thus gaily was ushered into the lady's life one of the most sinister phenomena in her history, the corset. The crime of establishing this instrument in its complete form is attributed—with so many lesser ones—to Catherine de' Medici. It was at any rate in full bloom under the later Valois. Montaigne has recorded his impression of it as he met it in society: *"Pour faire un corps bien espagnolé quelle gehenne les femmes ne souffrent-elles pas, guindées et sanglées avec de grosses coches sur les costes, jusques à la chair vive? Oui, quelquefois à en mourir."* And Ambrose Paré, who inspected its results on the dissecting table, remarked with interest in such fine ladies as came his way *"leur costes chevauchant les unes pardessus les autres."*

The effect of the tapering waist within the corset was reënforced by the expansion below the waist of the remarkable structure known as the farthingale, having the "bell-skirt" as a variant. With the distention of her lower section the lady lost practically all resemblance to a human being. The graceful female body, which had reminded so many poets of a slender amphora, took on the contour of the water-bottle. From the time of Francis the First to that of Queen Elizabeth the farthingale swelled unchecked. Ladies so different in temperament as Madame de Maintenon and Queen Victoria witnessed its vigorous revival. If we can determine from its career thus far the law that governs its appearance, we must say that it coincides with times that we call great. Antecedently improbable, it is nevertheless true that the ugliest, most meaningless and most fantastic dress ever donned by woman in Europe has prevailed in the great Minoan period of the Mediterranean civilisation, in the Renaissance, in the Elizabethan period, in the France that prepared the Revolution, in the England of the mid-Victorian giants and in the United States of the War for the Union.

If the lady's colouring and shape were treated with a somewhat high hand in the sixteenth century, there was an alarming increase in the means put at her disposal to make an artificial appeal to another sense than sight. The cleanliness of the middle-age had begun to decay. The sanitation of the new château was inferior to that of the Gothic donjon or abbey. Personal habits became astonishingly careless. As might have been expected, the art of the perfumer was in great demand. The lady of the time of Francis the First might be fragrant of violet powder, of Chypres, civet, musk, ambergris, orange-flowers, roses. She perfumed her gloves, her collars, her lace ruffles. Anything that she could do for society she did, short of the desperate step of the frequent bath.

Some of the minor details of her costume began to be strikingly modern. Watches were known early in the sixteenth century, under the name of "Nuremberg eggs." Under Henry the Second the egg became relatively flat and could be viewed in the light of an ornament. It brought the pocket in its wake, but for men only. Catherine de Medici is credited by Brantôme with another innovation more beneficent than the corset. She was, says he, *"la première qui ait mis la jambe dans l'arçon, d'autant que la grace y estoit plus belle et apparoissante que sur la planchette."* The *planchette* was the support slung at the right side of the horse or mule throughout the middle age, when the lady sat in her saddle as in a chair and made no pretension to control her mount. Of course many a lady was a true horsewoman in the olden time, but then apparently she rode astride and was somewhat exceptional; the adoption of the stirrup made her the rule.

The typical lady of the Renaissance was then in appearance formalised, bedevilled and bedisened, an apparition of somewhat stiffened splendour, a person in a pageant. Even in art she retains this character. Beatrice d'Este and

the Madonna at whose feet she kneels may
serve as types of the new and the old; but
sometimes, as in the painting known as "La
Belle Jardinière," the Madonna herself comes
very close to stays. The lady's real status in
this wonderful time was that of an object of art,
and this is perhaps her most logical aspect at
any time. It was certainly the most fortunate
aspect under which she could be considered in
that age, for the Renaissance knew not romance
and the sentimental lady, who might so easily
have been the next step after courteous love, did
wisely to postpone her appearance until the
strongly Latin impulse of the Revival had
worked itself out. Like every other object of
art, she was of course assigned her place in the
theories of art in general with which the time
abounded. Life itself was an art, for that matter, and the theory of it sprang from one generalisation to another with a somewhat dry
Latin lucidity, as if the whole field of human
experience had been laid out by Bramante.
There were taken up into this symmetrical conception of life a number of ideas which were
already familiar, and others which though not
new were so clipped and trimmed and combined
that their originators would not have recognised
them. One theme which appears in a variety of
forms, all bearing more or less directly on the

place of the lady in the composition, is the so-called "Platonism" of the Renaissance.

It is a familiar saying that every human being is born either a Platonist or an Aristotelian, though he may spend his life without becoming conscious of an offensive partisanship. At the time when the ideas were being formed that were to obsess the mind of mediæval Europe, the Platonic tendency as embodied in neo-Platonism was the prevailing one. Of the teaching of the neo-Platonists it may be said that they bore about the same relation to the words of Plato as the teachings of the early church bore to the words of Christ. Plotinus was almost as overwhelming a disciple as St. Paul. Each handed on in the name of the master a body of doctrine which the master would hardly have recognised. And, to make a very summary statement of a highly complicated matter, St. Augustine, taking his Platonism from Plotinus and his Christianity from St. Paul, gave currency to a system which, while showing at every turn the handiwork of Christ and of Plato, would certainly have surprised them both. The chief element foisted upon Plato by neo-Platonism was mysticism. Plato, though an enthusiast, kept his feet on the ground; but his enthusiasm was too much for weaker heads. To adapt the phrase of

Lady Macbeth, that which made him bold hath made them drunk. The ecstatic and the marvellous gat hold upon them and were highly congenial to the supernaturalism of the early church. The master's disparagement of the becoming as contrasted with the eternal became asceticism. Thus modified the ideas of Plato saturated the thought of the fathers, and his view of life, with a thousand crude applications, was a determining element in the *Weltanschauung* of the middle age. At first hand his doctrines were not known at all; the Latin translation of the Timæus by Chalcidius constituted for centuries the whole Platonic literature. And with the lapse of time the church went over to Aristotle. It is one of the ironies of history that when the true Plato, who had lent so formative a hand to Christianity, returned to Europe, he found Aristotle in possession of the field. He was just two hundred and fifty years too late. Nevertheless the unconscious Platonism of the middle age was irrepressible, and in one of its manifestations, running over into the Renaissance, it affected the lady nearly.

In a famous passage in the *Symposium* Socrates repeats what he professes to have heard from Diotima, the wise woman of Mantinea, on the subject of the higher mysteries of love:

"He who would approach this matter rightly must begin while he is young to frequent fair forms, and first, if his guide lead him aright, he must love one only of these forms and create thence fair discourse. Next he will notice that the beauty of any one form is akin to that of any other, and if the object of his search is bodily beauty, it would be folly not to recognise that the beauty of all bodies is one and the same. When he has arrived at this knowledge he will constitute himself the lover of all fair forms, despising as a petty thing his old vehement love for one. At the next stage he will hold that beauty in the soul is more honourable than beauty in the flesh, so that if a virtuous soul have but a little bloom, it will satisfy the lover to love and to tend him and to produce from him fair discourse, seeking such as will improve the young, until he is driven to take another step and behold the beauty of institutions and laws, and to realise that it is all akin and that bodily beauty is a very small matter. From the laws he will go to the sciences and seeing there beauty on the great scale he will no longer be enslaved by the beauty of the individual; but he will stand on the shore of the great sea of beauty and as he gazes he will become the father of many noble words and thoughts in his boundless love of wisdom. And finally, growing great and strong upon **that** shore, he will have a vision of a single science, which is the science of true beauty.

"Now try, if you please, to give me your very best attention. He whose education in love has been brought to this point, who beholds the beautiful in orderly succession, is now reaching the end and suddenly, Socrates, there will be revealed to him that wondrous beauty which has been the goal of all his efforts,—beauty which never begins nor ends, nor waxes nor wanes; not beauty which at any time or place or in any relation ceases to be beautiful, but which at all times and in all places and in all relations is fair; not beauty presenting itself under a masque as in a face or in hands or in speech or in science or in any other form; but beauty absolute, single, eternal. All other beautiful things share in some way this beauty, but while they are born and perish, true beauty grows neither greater nor less nor suffers any change.

"So when anyone by loving rightly rises from beautiful things and begins to perceive true beauty he will soon achieve his end. For the true progress of love is this, to begin with beautiful things and advance from them continually toward beauty itself, using them as rungs of the ladder, going from one fair form to two and from two to all, from fair forms to fair practices, thence to fair learning, and finally to that one science which is the knowledge of nothing but beauty itself. That is the life, my dear Socrates, if any there be, that a man should live, contemplating absolute beauty. You and many other men are enraptured by the sight of gold and raiment and beautiful boys and youths; you would go without meat and drink if you could and give all your time to gazing at them and enjoying their presence. But if once you were to see pure beauty you would not classify it with these things. What if it befell a man to behold it, simple, pure, unmixed, not choked with human flesh and blood and all the vanity of human life, but lonely and divine? Do you realise that there alone with it, beholding it with the eye of the mind, he will bring forth not vain images of virtue but virtue itself; and that a man who brings forth and cherishes true virtue is the friend of God and has eternal life?"

The discourse of Diotima in Plato's *Symposium* is easily recognised by those familiar with Plato's thought and style as highly characteristic of both. By the pretext of quoting the words of another, Socrates escapes from his ordinary colloquial dialectic and delivers a highly poetic oration. But his poetry is founded on a solid basis of logic. His theory of love is in rigorous agreement with his general doctrines both of the nature of things and of human knowledge. And while he contrives to fill with emotion what is at bottom a scientific statement, he so manages that neither his science nor his emotion is dogmatic save in form; the reader has leave to think for himself, to make a dozen inferences and applications, and to quarrel freely with the next reader over the author's meaning. Anyone who seizes the general drift of the passage will realise how much unconscious Platonism there was in the doctrine of courtesy, with its fundamental conception of the betterment of the lover by his love. Love is the source of all good, love is service, love kills pride, love dwells only in a *cor gentil,* love is an art,—all these maxims of courtesy can be found in pretty much the same words in one or another of the Platonic dialogues. As the theory rises in the hands of the Italians to its climax in Dante, it states ever more clearly that mortal beauty is a hint of God, and of God's vicegerent, philosophy. "I say and affirm," declares Dante, "that the lady by whom I am inspired with the highest love was the beautiful and honourable daughter of that governor of the world, to which Pythagoras gave the name of Philosophy." Beatrice is conscious of her function as representative of the highest good, for she says to herself:

"I miei disire,
Che ti menavano ad amar lo bene,
Di la dal qual non è a che si aspiri."

Thus in the height of the Aristotelian middle
age, its greatest poet lifted up the Platonic
torch, kindled heaven knows whence,—from
Cicero, from Boethius, from Chalcidius—and
burning with a strange flame that betrayed the
presence of much alloy in the fuel. But there
it was, a fresh expression of an old thought in
terms of a new view of life, bearing witness to
the soundness of the psychology which went so
deep into the human mind as to find there a law
equally operative in Athenian and mediævalist.
When Plato really came back to Europe the
cultivated world was eager to receive him; the
tradition was all aglow. But, immense as was
the advantage to posterity of his warm reception,
it had its drawback. The scholars of the
Renaissance were too full of their preconceived
notion of the master to receive his words on
their own merits. The fifteenth and the sixteenth centuries that talked so much of Plato
had the queerest ideas about him. They read
their own thoughts into his. They were after
all Latins and they might have said with Cotta
(as reported by Anatole France) *"J'aime beau-
coup le philosophie et je l'étudie à mes heures
de loisir. Mais je ne la comprends bien que*

dans les livres de Ciceron." Plato's theory of beauty was a godsend to a generation whose lives were governed by it,—of whom it was as true as it had been of the men of Hellas that "you would go without meat and drink if you could and give all your time to beholding and enjoying the presence of gold and of raiment and of beautiful young men." It was delightful to be assured that when one enjoyed the beauty of a golden cup or of a silken doublet, one was mounting upon the first rung of the ladder that leads to God. But by what different stages one passed up! Marsilio Ficino, the first Greek scholar of his time, Platonist-in-ordinary to Lorenzo the Magnificent, the benefactor of Europe in that he first translated the complete works of Plato into Latin and thus made them accessible to all, says in his introduction to the *Symposium:* "Now let us discuss the steps by which Diotima raised Socrates from the lowest by way of the intermediate, to the highest, drawing him from the body to the soul, from the soul to the angel, and from the angel to God."

Plato's doctrine of the supreme power of love owed its instant popularity and also the transformation it presently underwent to the same circumstance, namely the familiarity of polite Europe with other doctrines concerning the same matter. On the one hand stood the theory of courteous love and its widespread consequences. On the other side stood the author of the *Imitation of Christ,* saying for his part: "Nothing is sweeter than love, nothing more courageous, nothing higher, nothing wider, nothing more pleasant, nothing fuller nor better in heaven and earth; because love is born of God, and cannot rest but in God, above all created things. He that loveth, flieth, runneth and rejoiceth; he is free and is not bound. He giveth all for all and hath all in all, because he resteth above all things in one sovereign good, from which all that is good flows and proceeds. Love oftentimes knoweth no bounds, but is fervent beyond all measure. Love feels no burden, thinks nothing of trouble, attempts what is above its strength, pleads no excuse of impossibility; for it thinks all things lawful for itself and all things possible. If any man love, he knoweth what is the cry of this voice. For it is a loud cry in the ears of God, this ardent affection of the soul which saith, 'My God, my Love, thou art all mine and I am all thine.'"

People knew quite well that the "love" of the *Imitation* and the "love" of the *Chevalier de la Charrette* were two different things, and by all the mental habits of the middle age these two things were opposed. Each condemned the other. No means of reconciliation was dreamed of until suddenly it appeared that Plato had supplied a connecting link. But what was to Plato all one thing, a continuous road leading insensibly upward, was still to the men of the Renaissance two things, a lower floor and an upper with a ladder between them. Under the influence of this conception they believed with the best faith in the world that Plato taught the existence of two loves, the natural and the spiritual, and to the second alone they finally attached the epithet of "Platonic" *par excellence*. Thus a foreign idea was foisted upon Plato and was often enough the only definite doctrine associated with his name in the minds of people who did not read him; just as many persons to-day who have never read Darwin think of him as the man who said that we are descended from monkeys.

It did not really matter to the lady how what her age called Platonism was composed,—how many parts of Plato there were in it, to how many of Dionysius the Areopagite. Its main thesis was one of which she saw the practical value as applied to her own place in the scheme of things. Her *raison d'etre* was her character as a thing of beauty and object of love. To secure her dignity, beauty and love must both be nobly conceived. Diotima, who never mentioned a lady from first to last, nor, we may be sure, thought of one, furnished her with a complete apology for her existence. Granting that the female comes into the problem at all, she must be cultivated, free and gracious as well as comely,—in other words she must be a lady. Plato was felt to be essentially aristocratic. The homeliness of Socrates' speech, which shocked Montaigne even while it delighted him, did not disguise for Plato's Italian admirers his complete urbanity. Indeed among the many apparently accidental coincidences that made Plato the patron of the Renaissance must be placed high in the scale his unrivalled power of reproducing conversation, which fairly made him a text-book for a much-prized art. The talk of the Renaissance was one of the finest products of a period which in literature was not great, and in talk the lady shone, as she is always able to do when she will take the trouble. Her usually light equipment of learning is a positive advantage to her in conversation. If she cannot like Addison "draw for a thousand pounds," she can keep her sixpences readily accessible. The intellectual irresponsibility which she enjoys by consent, enables her to be paradoxical without losing credit and flippant without giving pain. To be brilliantly wrong and to submit gracefully to correction constitutes her greatest success. Her talk is not expected to inform but to stimulate. A man is handicapped by his inveterate habit of reference to the facts. To talk with another man is like playing for stakes, while to talk with a lady is merely playing for love. The lady virtually opens a conversation with the famous exordium of Rousseau: *"Commencons par écarter tous les faits."* Her business is with sentiment, emotion, manners, the comedy of life. To prove a general thesis she will adduce the romantic story of the friend of one of her friends. Yet though her thesis may have an insufficient inductive basis it is often true. It is the result of accumulated observations of which she is herself hardly aware and of which she could certainly give no account. Here lies her essential genius. When a literary talent accompanies it she bursts forth with a masterpiece like *Pride and Prejudice.* Such a woman as George Eliot who has a masculine taste for the positive is still at her best on her own ground. Her guesses, her "intuitions," are more valuable than her inductions. The modern lady is constantly tempted to leave her coign of vantage by the fact that life about her has often no social organisation at all in which her special gifts can be brought into play.   Only at certain times, of which perhaps the Renaissance is thus far the most noteworthy, will men join in the pursuit of an art of life.   The men of the Renaissance themselves started the game, and they found at once that the women were indispensable part-ners.

The lady of the Renaissance, seen in her most distinguished examples, has a great name for learning.   Italy, to begin with, was full of fe-male infant prodigies.   Some were daughters of learned men, like Dorothea Bucca, a doctor of the University of Bologna, and Alessandra Scala of Florence who composed Greek and Latin verses.   More were daughters of great houses like Cecilia Gonzaga, daughter of the Duke of Mantua, Paula Malatesta, Isabella Sforza and the great Vittoria Colonna.   From Italy the fashion spread in every direction. Lady Jane Grey was reading Plato in the orig-inal when she was thirteen; at the same age Mary Stuart delivered her Latin oration at the court of France; Queen Elizabeth at fourteen translated the *Mirror of the Sinful Soul,* a famous work by Margaret of France.   The career of Olympia Morata illustrates the cos-mopolitanism of the phenomenon.   She was the pupil first of her scholarly father, then, at the court of Ferrara, of the most learned men of her

time. At fourteen she was writing a eulogy of
Cicero in Latin, of Mucius Scaevola in Greek,
speaking both languages, giving public lectures.
When she married Gruntler, a German physician, and threw in her lot with the reformers,
Italy became too hot to hold her, but she continued to live the learned life at Wurzburg and
at Heidelberg, accepted as an equal by the men
of letters, in a land where in general the lady
was still at the needlework stage. In practice
this alarming spread of erudition among female
children was apparently confined to the well-to-
do and noble. And Jean Bouchet laid down the
theory, in defending a learned lady: "Some find
it strange," says he, " that this lady employs her
mind in composing books, saying that this is not
the business of her sex. But this superficial
judgment proceeds from ignorance, for in discussing such pursuits we must distinguish
among women, according to their birth and
estate. It is my opinion that women of low
condition who must needs busy themselves with
familiar and domestic matters, should not occupy
themselves with learning, which is a matter
repugnant to rusticity. But queens, princesses
and other ladies who have men-servants and
maids to relieve them of vulgar tasks will do
much better to use their minds and time in good
and honourable study than in dancing and feast-

ing." The ancients, he adds, abounded in learned women, and among Christian ladies he cites St. Jerome's Paula, St. Catherine whose science confounded the doctors, and *"toutes les Sibilles."*

If learning began early with the girls of the Renaissance, so did the rest of life. Anne of France fell in love at the age of ten. St. Theresa's emotions (she tells us) began to sway her when she was six and she had run away twice before she was twenty. Vivès, the great Spanish educator, based his theory of education not on the nature of the ideal young girl, but of the young girl as he saw her. "The craters of Etna," he said, "cannot vie with the fires of the temperament of a young girl inflamed by high feeding." To control these flames Vivès proposed a vegetable diet and a classical education, harmonised with a little domestic science. His method seemed impregnable. If anyone objected that learning makes women irreligious, he could point to the prominent place occupied in his curriculum by Biblical exegesis. If the objection was that a learned lady makes a bad housewife, he boasted that with the scientific training he recommended, his pupils would be the most intelligent of cooks and nurses. Vivès went to England with Catherine of Aragon and started the ball rolling

there. The practical and manly character of
his education is reflected in the mental habits
of the great Elizabeth herself. But in Italy it
was still borne in mind that the lady's business
is to charm. Plain cooking should not be
thought of among her accomplishments but
learning was essential. "A little girl," said
Bembo, "ought to learn Latin; it completes her
charm." And Greek did not hurt her. Her
reading was chosen with a view to exciting and
refining her sensibility; Virgil, parts of Horace,
Dante, Petrarch, Bembo and Castiglione were
suggested. She was to face love, to realise its
two aspects and to learn to choose the better
and reject the worse. Melancholy was to be
banished by learning and the pursuit of beauty.
No allowance was made for the sense of humour.
In France on the other hand, melancholy was
banished by laughter. It has been said that
Rabelais was the Michelangelo of France. It
is astonishing to learn what the young ladies of
that land laughed at in the fifteenth and sixteenth
centuries. Some of the *Colloquies* of Erasmus
that were written especially for the young contained passages that, among others, caused the
collection to be censured by the Sorbonne,
placed on the Index at Rome and burned in
Spain. The famous flea, perceived on the
bosom of Mlle. des Roches and celebrated in

song by Scaliger and Turnebus, by Brisson and
de Harley, has served in the hands of Sainte
Beuve to characterise the intellectual society of
the time.   But it is only a flea and can be
swallowed; the real strain comes when one
catches sight of the camel, as in the tales listened
to and told by the young ladies of the Heptameron.   These tales cannot justly be called im-
moral.   On the contrary, when they touch on
morals at all they refer to a wholesome and
sometimes even to a noble standard.   The
wicked friar always comes to grief and generally (which is worse) to ridicule.   What gives
them their rakish air is the fact that the ladies
are frankly and manfully amused by the indec-
orous, and the youngest lady is the frankest.
France was already the home of the *demi-vierge*.
Modern society draws two fairly sharp lines
through the mass of womankind, dividing it into
three groups.   In the first group are the women
who will neither hear nor speak the unconven-
tional; in the second the women who will hear
it but will not speak it; in the third the women
who will both hear and speak.   On the evidence
of the *Heptameron* there were no such lines in
the France of Francis the First.   One reason
may have been the fact that girls were taught
by men.   A great deal is explained in the case
of Margaret of France when we reflect that

she received her education from a tutor precisely as her brother did and very likely in his company. The governess seems to have been disapproved of even by professed admirers of the feminine mind. "I allow woman to learn," said Bruno; "to teach, never." The domestic tutor had his drawbacks. Brantôme had a poor opinion of him, saying that he abused his professional opportunities, and that when he was obliged to read the Bible with his pupils he selected the most *risqué* passages. No such criticism could apply to Vivès, tutor of princesses as well as of princes, whose ideas were austere. He disapproved of what we call "fiction" as reading for young girls. The romances outraged both morals and logic; they had no reasonable relation to life. Erasmus, on the contrary, as we have seen, so thoroughly believed in light literature for the young that he prepared some himself. Anne of France too, another educational authority, believed in a special literature *pour la jeunesse*, and has left us a dreary example from her own pen,—a tale founded on a tragic episode in Froissart, where a father has to betray his military trust or allow his son to be murdered by the English. Virtue triumphs, the father does his duty, the mother swoons, the son is executed. Sunday-school fiction is inaugurated.

II

IN all these differences of opinion among those entitled to have an opinion we have the very breath of the Renaissance. The middle age as we see it looks very like a bed with too many people in it, where all must turn over at once. In the centuries that followed people had somehow plucked up courage to demand rooms to themselves. The only general statements that can safely be made concerning the lady of those centuries are those which explain that generalisation is no longer possible.

The most satisfactory way to study her under the new condition is to take one or two concrete examples, assured that any such will expand beneath our eyes and establish for us any number of relations with all sorts of matters. For if we are not at liberty to generalize about that society, it never wearied of generalising about itself.

Mr. Lowes Dickinson has lately given the world a fresh impression of the value and charm of the philosophic dialogue, a literary form which, like the epistolary novel, has its obvious dangers and is for the most part, perhaps wisely, looked upon askance. As Mr. Dickinson uses it, with a new content, it carries associations of a purely formal sort, primarily of course with

Plato. It must be said, I think, that while the Plato-lover is always glad to be reminded of Plato, it is more magnanimous than wise in a modern author to evoke that great shade too vividly as a standard of comparison. But the reader of the *Modern Symposium* as he closes the book with the last speaker's confession of faith in his ears and the vision of early morning before his eyes, is reminded, more legitimately than of Plato, of another great dialogue which closes also with a hymn, and with the discovery that "a beautiful dawn of rosy hue was already born in the east, and that all the stars had vanished save Venus, sweet mistress of the sky, who holds the bonds of night and day; from which there seemed to breathe a gentle wind that filled the air with crisp coolness and began to waken sweet choruses of joyous birds in the murmuring forests of the hills hard by." * In this dialogue Count Baldesar Castiglione, setting out to describe the perfect courtier, gives us incidentally a treatise on the lady of his day, her theory and practice, together with a magnificent statement of the doctrine of Platonic love.

Federico di Montefeltro built in the fifteenth

* The Courtier. Translated by Mr. L. E. Opdycke. The succeeding paragraphs are chiefly a condensation from Mr. Opdycke's version.

century on the rugged site of Urbino a palace
regarded by many as the most beautiful to be
found in all Italy; and he so well furnished it
with everything suitable that it seemed not a
palace but a city in the form of a palace,—
silver vases, hangings of richest cloth-of-gold,
antique statues, pictures most choice, and a
goodly number of most excellent and rare books
in Greek, Latin and Hebrew. This duke,
dying gloriously as he had lived, was succeeded
by his only son, Guidobaldo, infirm of body but
great in spirit, who married Madonna Elisa-
betta Gonzaga and gathered about him a
household of very noble talents. The house
could truly be called the very abode of mirth;
for, not to speak of the honour it was to each
to serve such a lord, there was born in the hearts
of all a supreme contentment in the presence of
the duchess, where also was ever to be found
the lady Emilia Pia, sister-in-law to the duke,
but widowed though young. She was endowed
with such lively wit and judgment that everyone gained wisdom and worth from her. She
it was who one evening when the company had
gathered as usual about the duchess, started a
game in which we may see the offspring of the
Courts of Love which used to entertain the
middle age. Discussion was still dear, and
Emilia's game consisted in requiring each

gentleman present to propose a topic. Many and tempting were the suggestions. My lord Gaspar Pallavicino who, whether in sport or earnest, professed to think lightly of ladies, proposed that each should tell what virtue he would have of all others in the person beloved and also, since all must have some blemish, what fault he would have in her. Another would hear from each, if she whom he loves must need be angry with him, by what cause he would have her anger roused. Another would hear from each, if she whom he loves must need be angry with him, from which he would have her anger spring, her fault or his own. These and other proposals were defeated by the suggestion that one of the company should be selected to describe the Perfect Courtier, and after two evenings had been spent in carrying out this plan, the charge was laid upon Giuliano de' Medici to describe the perfect Court Lady.

Giuliano admitted at the outset that certain qualities were equally desirable in man and woman, such as prudence, magnanimity and continence; and that certain others were desirable in all women alike, such as kindness, discretion and housewifery. The special characteristic of a lady who lives at court should be a certain pleasant affability, whereby she may be able to entertain politely every sort of man with

agreeable converse; she should unite with calm
and modest manners a quick vivacity of spirit
whereby she may show herself alien to all in-
delicacy, and she must preserve a certain mean
(difficult and composed almost of contraries)
and must barely touch certain limits but not
pass them. Thus she ought not to be so coy
and seem so to abhor company and talk that are
a little free, as to take her leave as soon as she
finds herself therein; nor ought she, on the other
hand, for the sake of showing herself free and
agreeable, to utter unseemly words; but when
she is present at such talk, she ought to listen
with a little blush.

The question of the lady's exercise brought
out opposed opinions, each based on æsthetic
considerations. Some had seen ladies play
tennis, handle weapons, ride, go hunting and
perform nearly all the exercises that a cavalier
can. Accolti boldly regretted that with many
other good old customs we have lost that of the
ancients which permitted women to wrestle un-
clothed with men. But Giuliano de' Medici
would have none of this. His lady must not
practice the rugged exercises of men; even in
dancing she must not use too violent movements,
but the circumspection and gentle daintiness
that befits her. Nor in singing or playing
should she employ those abrupt diminutions

which show more skill than sweetness. Imagine how unlovely it would be to see a woman play drum, fife or trumpet!

The lady should carefully consider her dress, since she must take care for beauty, and beauty is of divers sorts. She should study her style, both of soul and body, and dress accordingly. And the lady should have knowledge of letters, music, painting. And thus, in her talk, her laughter, her play, she will be very graceful and will entertain appropriately whoever comes before her.

My lord Gaspar then said, laughing: "Since you have given women letters and continence and magnanimity and temperance, I only marvel that you would not also have them govern cities, make laws and lead armies, and let the men stay at home to cook or spin."

Giuliano replied, also laughing; "Perhaps even this would not be amiss."

But my lord Gaspar believed that since nature always aims to make things most perfect, she would continually bring forth men if she could; and when a woman is born, it is a mistake or defeat of nature, as in the case of one that is born blind or halt. Moreover (he asks) why is it that a woman always loves her first lover, while a man soon hates his first mistress? Surely because the woman receives perfection from the man, and the man imperfection from the woman, and everyone naturally loves what makes him perfect and hates what makes him imperfect. He explains the high value set upon "virtue" in women by the fact that when that goes their whole worth goes, for the world has no good from women except the bearing of children.

While the main argument rests in the hands of the men of the party, who muster on one side or the other all the accumulated ideas of their day in a blend of theology, courteous love and neo-Platonism, the ladies are allowed, by the art of the dialogue, to be seen in the act of governing society. Castiglione is not content to label his pet, Emilia Pia, witty, charming and endowed with judgment; he does a much more difficult thing and shows her actually to be so. The part she played at Urbino as lieutenant to the duchess suggests from some points of view the rôle of Julie de Lespinasse. But in this case there was no treachery. Emilia was a faithful friend in dark days as well as fair, accompanied her duchess into exile, and, surviving her, was her executrix. She was unquestionably one of the great artists of the Renaissance, but an artist in a perishable medium, like an opera-singer. Castiglione at the beginning of his third book says that as

Pythagoras discovered the measure of Hercules' body from the measure of his foot, so the reader may judge of the preëminence of the court of Urbino by this glimpse of its amusements. In the same way we may measure the genius of Emilia and the duchess by the record of a single evening. Having between them kept the men in play, and caused a great deal of good talk to be uttered without weariness, they changed the key and desired two of the ladies to dance. Whereupon a very charming musician began to play upon his instruments; and joining hands the two ladies performed first a Spanish dance and then a French one, with consummate grace and to the great delight of those who saw them.

One of the guests at Urbino during these famous four days was Pietro Bembo, afterwards cardinal, the Peter on whom, as Professor Fletcher says, was founded the new religion of beauty, and who had published for it in that very year one of the earliest of its gospels, *Gli Asolani*. At the end of the fourth evening my lord Gaspar Pallavicino, always fertile in difficulties, raised an interesting one. It was apparent that the perfect courtier would not be a young man, for the worth and authority by which he was to allure his prince are inevitably the fruit of years. On the other hand, it had been settled that he would be a lover. Now, how becoming is it for a man no longer young to be in love? Is there not danger that the lover will forget to instruct his prince, and that his follies will make him a laughing-stock?

Bembo was on his feet instantly,—this was his subject. There are two ways of loving. If the courtier choose the better way, he would get no blame but much praise and highest happiness unaccompanied by any pain, which rarely and almost never happens with young men.

The duchess immediately laid upon him the task of teaching the courtier this love which is so happy that it brings with it no pain; and Bembo, having first remained silent awhile, then settled himself a little as if about to speak of something important, and began at last to speak, playfully at first but with a growing earnestness and eloquence which ended in a burst of pure enthusiasm.

According to the definition of the ancient sages (said messer Pietro) love is naught but a certain desire to enjoy beauty. The beauty we have especially in mind is an effluence of divine goodness, diffused like the sun's light upon all created things, yet when it finds a face well proportioned and framed with a certain pleasant harmony of various colours, it infuses itself therein and appears most beautiful, like a sunbeam falling upon a vase of gold set with

precious gems. Thus it agreeably attracts the
eyes of men, and thereby entering the soul stirs
her with a new sweetness and excites in her a
desire for its own self. Then if the soul allows
herself to be guided by the judgment of sense,
she runs into very grievous errors, and judges
that the body wherein the beauty is seen is the
chief cause thereof; whoever thinks to enjoy the
beauty by possessing the body deceives himself.
Hence all those lovers who satisfy their desires
with the women they love, love most unhappily;
for either they never attain their desires (which
is great unhappiness) or if they do attain
thereto, they find they have attained their woe.
Such lovers are young men in general, but the
contrary happens to those of mature years; if
they are inflamed by beauty, they are not de-
ceived. Therefore their possession of it always
brings them good; because beauty is good, and
hence true love of beauty is most good and holy.
Beauty springs from God. A wicked soul
rarely inhabits a beautiful body. Look at the
state of this great fabric of the world, the round
firmament adorned with so many lights. These
things have such influence upon one another
that if they were changed for an instant they
could not hold together and would wreck the
world; they have also such beauty and grace
that human wit cannot imagine anything more

beautiful. Much praise is therefore bestowed
on everything in the world by saying that it is
beautiful, and we may say that the good and
the beautiful are the same thing, and especially
in the human body; of whose beauty I think the
most immediate cause is beauty of the soul.
To enjoy beauty without suffering there is need
that the courtier should, with the aid of reason,
wholly turn his desire from the body to the
beauty alone. In this wise he will be beyond
all the bitterness that the young nearly always
feel. He will do no injury to the husband or
the kinsfolk of the beloved lady; he will put
no infamy upon her. But he will find another
blessing greater still if he will employ this love
to mount to one much higher,—if he will no
longer contemplate the particular beauty of one
woman, but that universal beauty which adorns
all bodies. And just as love leads the soul
from the particular to the universal beauty, so
in the highest stage it leads her from the particular to the universal intellect. Hence the
soul, kindled by the most sacred fire of true
divine love, flies to unite herself with the angelic
nature; changed into an angel, she understands
all things intelligible, and without veil or cloud
views the wide sea of pure divine beauty.

What mortal tongue, then, O most holy Love,
can praise thee worthily? Accept our souls

which are offered to thee in sacrifice; burn them
in that living flame which consumes all mortal
dross, to the end that, being wholly separated
from the body, they may unite with divine
beauty by a perpetual and very sweet bond, and
that we may at last die a most happy and living
death, as died of old those ancient fathers whose
souls thou, by the most glowing power of contemplation, didst ravish from the body and unite
with God.

Having thus spoken Bembo remained silent
awhile as if in ecstasy, and the company with
him, until at last the lady Emilia, gently pluck-
ing him by the border of his robe, said: "Have
a care, messer Pietro, that with these thoughts
your soul also does not forsake your body."

"My lady," replied messer Pietro, "that
would not be the first miracle that love has
wrought upon me."

III

VERGERIO, the pope's nuncio in France,
gives praise to Jesus Christ for the
great ladies of his time, Vittoria
Colonna at Rome, Leonora Gonzaga at Urbino,
Renée of France at Ferrara, and Margaret,
Queen of Navarre. The lady named last was so
obliging as to compose in her person, her life and

works, a strongly representative figure of the Renaissance in France, and to afford in particular some striking instances of its likeness and unlikeness to the Renaissance in Italy. Margaret who is known to posterity chiefly as the foster-mother if not the actual parent of a collection of scandalous tales, was in her own day regarded as a very serious person. Vittoria Colonna felt for her a religious awe; she writes that when she thinks of Margaret she is filled with the same fear that seized the Israelites when they saw the glory of God revealed in fire on the mountain-top. Clément Marot spoke of her as "woman in body, man in heart, angel in head." She was profoundly interested in religion and wrote continually upon its problems,—*The Mirror of the Sinful Soul, The Strife between Flesh and Spirit,* and *The Orison of Jesus Christ.* A faithful Catholic to the end, she belonged to the group who were reformers before the Reformation, founding and encouraging the ideas that were to horrify them by their logical consequences, precisely as polite society in the eighteenth century played with the ideas of the Revolution. The *Mirror* was censured by the Sorbonne as unorthodox, and but for the forcible intervention of the king, her brother, a princess of France would have been banned as a heretic. In her castle of Nérac many a reformer found protection from ecclesiastical persecution.

Margaret's education had of course been the work of a tutor, Robert Hurault, Baron of Auzay and Abbot of St. Martin of Autun. With this worthy man she read Latin and French, Spanish and Italian, but although she could speak good Spanish and good Italian, Brantôme says that she always made use of her mother-tongue for matters of moment. It is said that she also had some lessons in Hebrew, and when the time came to pronounce her funeral oration Sainte-Marthe was ready to affirm that she had been instructed by the most learned men of her time in the philosophical principles of the ancients. She has been celebrated more recently as a Platonist and the cause of Platonism in others, a student herself of the master's philosophy and influential in introducing it as an element of the French Renaissance. It is quite true that Margaret's religion and her theory of love, her verses and her tales, are full of the mystic neo-Platonism that we have already noted as diffused in the middle age and concentrated in the Renaissance; but the reader will do well to remember here as in other cases the difference between Plato seen through a glass darkly and Plato seen face to face. All that is Platonic in Margaret's

writings could have been supplied easily by
Petrarch and Bembo between them, and there
is no need to credit her with a first-hand knowledge of the master for which there seems to be
no direct evidence.

The *Heptameron* has thus much in common
with the *Courtier* that it shows us a group of
men and women of the best society, under the
presidency of a very great lady indeed (if, as
seems likely, Oisille represents Margaret's
mother, Louise of Savoy,) organising a game
for the purpose of refined and edifying entertainment.   It must not be decided off-hand that
Margaret's definition of these adjectives was
altogether different from Castiglione's, for an
earlier draft of the *Courtier* shows that the
published text has been considerably Bowdler-
ised.   Still it is but fair to compare final
form with final form, and as they both stand,
the *Courtier* is a far more ladylike work than
the tales of the Queen of Navarre.   In
Margaret's book however the greatest inde-
corum is confined precisely to the tales, which
are the less original part.   The dialogue,
which is in some lights the more interesting
portion, does not reveal a different standard
from that of the Italian.   Apart from what is
after all but a question of manners, the two
books agree in a very fundamental matter

They both show a society of men and women keenly interested in the same subjects, namely the complexities of social life and especially of the relation therein of the sexes to each other. Both in other words rest on the assumption that social life is an art. On this assumption and on this only the lady's importance is equal to that of the gentleman. The economic question fades out and the physiological question becomes subordinate. The antagonism of sex remains but it is no longer actual war; the foils are buttoned. The elementary problems of existence have been solved; in their place stand the questions arising out of the postulates of social convention. Here the lady not only has her rights but she is indispensable. Her point of view is listened to with interest. If the comparison may be permitted, Margaret's view of the province and function of fiction is precisely that of Mr. Henry James. Mr. James and all his contemporaries have the misfortune to live in an age when but a very small portion of society is interested in the pursuit of happiness under the forms of art. In Margaret's day everyone was interested in it; it really mattered. To the lady, herself the creation of art, it was her vital air, though she did not realise this until some centuries later when it began to be pumped out. Believing

that her universe was stable and her place therefore assured, she used it as the basis of a by no
means ignoble theory of her rights and duties.

The group of travellers who found themselves
detained at the Abbey of Our Lady of Serrance
by the flood of the river Gave arranged an
interesting programme to help them through
the tedious days. Early in the morning they
repaired to the room of the aged lady Oisille
and listened for an hour to her reading of the
scriptures; then piously heard mass, and went
to dinner at ten o'clock. After dinner each retired to his room to meditate and prepare his
contribution to the afternoon's entertainment.
At noon the company assembled in a pleasant
meadow by the riverside, where trees gave
abundant shade and the grass was soft and thick
to sit upon. After each day's quota of tales was
told the company went to vespers. The first
day they found they had kept the monks waiting a full hour or more. On the second day
when they repaired to the church they found
that although the vesper-bell had rung there
was not a single monk present to say the office.
"The monks, indeed, had heard that the company assembled in the meadow to tell the
pleasantest tales imaginable, and being fonder
of pleasure than of their prayers, they had gone
and hidden themselves in a ditch, where they

lay flat on their bellies behind a very thick hedge; and they had there listened so eagerly to the stories that they had not heard the monastery bell, as was soon clearly shown, for they returned in such great haste that they almost lacked breath to begin the saying of vespers."

This combination of piety and irreverence, of interest in the scriptures, obedience to the ritual of the church and contempt for the monk, casts various lights on the frame of mind of society just before the Reformation. Religion bore on life with a naïveté that we are generally inclined to attribute to the heathen alone. "They proceeded to the contemplation of the mass, when one and all commended themselves to the Holy Ghost in order that they might that day be enabled to satisfy their merry audience." One of the ladies told the story of an amour of Francis the First, "a prince that feared and loved God." He found that a short-cut to the house of the lady he loved took him through a monastery, and although he made no pause in going, he never failed on his return to continue for a long time praying in the church. This famous anecdote is a summary of the interplay of love and religion that was characteristic of Margaret's own mind. It sounds more edifying when Parlamente puts it in her charming way:

"I believe no man can ever love God perfectly
that has not perfectly loved one of his creatures
in this world." That is the sort of thing the
Queen's admirers have in mind when they call
her a Platonist. In a delightful tale that
(almost inadvertently) celebrates the break-
down of "Platonic love," in real life, Margaret
anticipates the lady-novelist of later times in
framing the sort of declaration that the lady is
always thirsting to hear. Amadour, enamoured
of a young gentlewoman betrothed to a king's
son, addresses her thus: "I know that I cannot
marry you, and even if I could, I would not
do so in the face of the love you bear him whom
I would fain see your husband. And as for
loving you with a vicious love like those who
hope that long service will bring them a reward to the dishonour of a lady, that is far from
my purpose. I would rather see you dead than
know that you were less worthy of being loved,
or that your virtue had diminished for the sake
of any pleasure to me. For the end and reward
of my service I ask but one thing, namely that
you will be so faithful a mistress to me as
never to take your favour from me, and that
trusting in me more than in any other, and
accepting from me the assurance that if for
your honour's sake, or for aught concerning you,

you ever have need of a gentleman's life, I will gladly place mine at your disposal."

Unlike the *Courtier,* the *Heptameron* exhibits the ladies themselves doing a great deal of the talking. Castiglione's ladies are chiefly occupied in drawing out the men. Nor is the difference a merely accidental one between two books. In Italy where the Renaissance was autochthonous it was the work of men, and the lady fell in with the current. In France where it was largely a matter of importation, the lady's judgment and taste were part of the conditions that determined its form. Nor did she let go the hold it offered her. During the two succeeding centuries in which France organised civilised life for Europe the lady was assigned an important role. She succeeded unluckily in identifying herself with a self-destructive social mechanism, but while it lasted her position was strong. She gathered up and combined all that Christianity, Teutonism, courtesy, art and convention had contributed for her benefit, and by their means developed a type which reminded Schopenhauer of "the holy apes of Benares, who in the consciousness of their sanctity and inviolable position, think they can do exactly as they please."

THE LADY OF THE SALON

I

"Je vous ai recommandé cent fois la vertu; mais n'allez pas attacher a ce mot une foule d'idées puériles et ridicules. Je ne reconnais dans une femme d'autre sagesse que celle qui convient à un honnête homme." MADAME DE PUYSIEUX, *Conseils à Une Amie*.

TOWARDS the end of the reign of Henry the Fourth of France, the Marquise de Rambôuillet built for herself a new hôtel in the Rue St. Thomas-du-Lovre, and placed her staircase in a corner of the building instead of in the middle where all the world had supposed a staircase must be. The social significance of this innovation was quickly seized and applied by other ladies. When the Queen Mother built the Luxembourg she sent her architects to look at the Hôtel Rambôuillet. Perhaps the famous influence of that house upon French life and letters would have been the same with a central staircase, but the genius that exerted the one expressed itself not less significantly in the abolition of the other. The central staircase had cut the house in two, with an enormous drawing-room on one side and an enormous bedroom on the other. No one had conceived a less naïve distribution. Mme. de Rambôuillet took the first step towards the humanisation of the hôtel. Many more remained to be taken, but they followed inevitably from hers. Having recovered from the staircase the central section of her house, she could arrange the whole floor in a suite of communicating rooms, throwing them together or separating them at will by a system of folding-doors symmetrically arranged. In working out her main idea she added some highly agreeable details, loftier ceilings, larger windows and a livelier scheme of decoration. Before her day no one had thought of painting walls with any other colour than red or tan; she invented her famous blue room. So much of the tradition of the donjon and its furniture remained that the chief mobile feature of the blue room was the great bed in its alcove which the lady occupied to receive her guests,—the *lit paré* of a hundred contes of the middle age.

Throughout the reign of Louis the Fourteenth, this theory of the house prevailed, modified of course by the temperament of that monarch. Rooms grew larger and larger; it was impossible to heat them in winter. Furniture grew more and more monumental; it was impossible to be at ease in one's chair. In all this, the changing aspect of the lady was implied. She no longer sat upon the grass with jolly Queen Margaret. She was indeed even after the Renaissance accepted and understood as an object of art, but the art of the grand monarch was architecture, for which the lady was an uncongenial and even refractory medium. She became portentous. Her dress was magnificent, stiff, ponderous, inhuman. The portraiture of the time shows her heroic size, her hard Olympian physiognomy. The passions she inspired were formidable and unwieldy, systematically developed and expressed, in a word, baroque.

There is hardly a more striking instance in the lady's history of the reaction between her and her physical surroundings than the complete change in domestic architecture and art that marked the opening of the regency and of an age of feminism, at the beginning of the lady's great century. The dowager Duchess de Bourbon built in 1722 an hôtel which embodied the new spirit, and the eighteenth century was launched. Pierre Patti, an architect of the reign of Louis the Fifteenth understood the matter very well. "Nothing does us so much honour as the invention of the art of distributing apartments. Before us the one consideration was the exterior and magnificence;

the interiors were vast and inconvenient. There were drawing-rooms two stories high and spacious reception-rooms. . . . All these were placed end to end without detachment. Houses were solely for publicity, not for private comfort. All the pleasant arrangements that we admire to-day in the new hôtels, the artful detachment of rooms, the concealed staircases so convenient for hiding an intrigue or avoiding importunate visitors, those contrivances that lighten the labour of servants and make our houses delightful and enchanted dwellings, all these are the invention of our day." With the smaller and more personal room, there came naturally a different theory of decoration. The ponderous disappeared. The timbers which used to be allowed their decorative value were hidden by ceilings and panels. The colossal was replaced by the little. The statues, the columns, the great canvases made way for china figurines, for carven garlands and for mirrors. If the gentlemen of France breathed more freely when Louis the Fourteenth was dead, the lady's emancipation needs a stronger figure. She was herself again; powers had been accumulating for her as money accumulates for an heir during his minority; her great century was before her; and the first outward result of her action was to diminish the scale. Her furniture was not henceforward to make her look dwarfed; she was tired of the rôle of an ill-executed caryatid. The grandiose and the symmetrical had never become her; her ardent wish was to be surrounded with small objects and to get rid, as far as possible, of things with two sides alike.

The lady's history has in all times been reflected and symbolised by that of her garden. The legend that associates our first mother with a natural garden and Demeter with the fruits of the earth has a meaning that deepens rather than fades as the woman becomes a lady and gardening becomes a fine art. In both the lady and the garden something primarily useful is maintained unproductively for its æsthetic value alone. In each case protoplasm is moulded and coloured by art like so much wax or plaster. The two creations are always felt to be akin; the lady is at her best in the garden, and the garden is incomplete without the lady. It represents the social process that has made her possible; the exclusion of hurtful influences, the repression and modification of natural forces, the pleasant sense of refinement that comes of spending money and labour in the production of the palpably useless. The age that produces an incontestably new type of lady is as proud of it as the gardener can be of a new double or scented variety. The eighteenth century saw many startling vicissitudes of gardening, and the ladies it produced were comparable only with the black tulip and the blue rose. Art could do no more.

The great garden of the seventeenth century was a man's garden, logical, disciplined, derived in all its details from one controlling principle, planned on an enormous scale. Every gentleman's lawn exhibited a miniature Versailles. The politics and the finance of the reign were mirrored in its gardens. Le Notre and Colbert were but different manifestations of the same genius. Their works had the same duty to fulfil toward their common master, to praise him and magnify him forever. It is true that Louis wavered for a moment between Le Notre's plan and that of Dufresney. Dufresney had designed for the Abbé Pajot a natural garden (as the seventeenth century conceived the natural) without a straight line in it.

But the King after due consideration gave a pension to Dufresney and adopted the plan of Le Notre. He perceived that the natural garden would be a contradiction of the spirit of his reign. Among his subjects it had a certain brief vogue and then died out in France. When it revived there after nearly a century it came in congenial company with the rights of man and the maternal nourishment of infants, Anglomania and the hankering after a bicameral constitution. But across the channel it was immediately adopted and was the starting point of what we know as the English garden. In the meantime the ideas of Le Notre prevailed in France. It was an age of long reigns. The new hôtels of the early eighteenth century preserved his formalities, his uncompromising pursuit of a principle. It was bound in the long run to go down before Rousseau and the return to nature, but it began by lending itself to the first aims of the simple life. It was easy to arrange a bit of *bergerie* in a corner of a symmetrical garden by installing a terracotta shepherd and shepherdess and clipping the box-trees into sheep. Retarded somewhat by such adaptations, the revolution nevertheless came at last. Men's politics expressed themselves in their gardens; some were called English and some were called Chinese, though in fact they looked very much alike. The main thing was to get rid of symmetry, which was identified with the old régime.

The lady's own personal appearance in the eighteenth century is set before us by exceptionally full documents. It is true that a certain allowance must be made in studying the portrait of the lady in any age. It is well known that she exerts a strong and characteristic influence on every functionary who exists to supply her special wants, so that a ladies' doctor is readily distinguishable from other doctors, and the cashier in a ladies' bank from other cashiers. In a much greater degree is the professional painter of ladies' portraits distinguishable from other portrait painters. It is only the painters primarily of men, like Velasquez and Rembrandt, who give us the ladies of their time in their frank and engaging ugliness. But if the painter of ladies cannot be trusted to tell us exactly how his sitters really looked, he tells us something far more important. We know à priori that as far as flesh and blood and eyes and teeth go, they looked like their counterparts in any age. What the painter tells is something we could not have learned from any other source, and what the lady's painter always tells, how, namely, the sitter wished to look. Where the man's talent is great, it would perhaps be more just to say that his canvas shows how he wishes the sitter looked; but his ideal and the sitter's are generally the same. Her dress and her jewels are sure to be faithfully presented; if the length of her legs and the curve of her lips are theoretical, and indeed appear to be nearly uniform at any given period, we are told the truth at one remove, we are put in possession of the ideal of a society.

One of the briefest ways to describe the ideal of a lady's appearance in the eighteenth century is to say that the pastel was invented to express it. Nothing could so conclusively stamp it a woman's century as the rise and prevalence of this medium, itself the invention of a woman. The soft bloom of the lady's cheek, the gentle brilliance of her eyes, the light luxuriance of her hair, the tender colours and graceful fabrics of her dress, the characteristic sentiment of her whole appearance are recalled to us at once by the mere mention of the pastel. It carries with it a whole theory of manners, of love and life. To prove the degree to which it affects the imagination, it is necessary only to study one of Gainesborough's or Romney's ladies skilfully copied in pastel and to note the inexplicable oddity of the transformation. It is true that the whole thing was manfully launched by Watteau in oils. That singular genius doubtless contributed more than any one man to determine the lady's idea of herself until she fell under the even more strongly suggestive influence of Rousseau. But the pastel raised Watteau's view of life to the second power. What he contrived by a miracle to do with oils could be done quite naturally with pastels. The transition under the Regency from the positiveness of the last reign to the sentimentalism of the next is embodied in them. The Goncourts with their agreeable rhetoric of over-statement have expressed this change in a passage that cannot be forgotten:

"But already," they say, "in the midst of the deities of the Regency appeared a type more delicate, more expressive. A beauty quite different from the beauties of the Palais-Royal begins to make itself felt in that little lady, whose bust-portrait by Rosalba hangs in the Louvre. How charming is the firm and slender grace of this figure! The delicate complexion recalls the fairness of Saxe porcelain, the black eyes light up the whole face; the nose is fine, the mouth small, the neck slender and long. There is no show of dress, no operatic properties; nothing but a bouquet at the breast and a garland of natural flowers interwoven with the loose curls of her hair. It is a new grace making her appearance, who seems, even with the little grimacing monkey held against her by her slender fingers, to proclaim the irregular features and charms that were to fascinate the century. Little by little, woman's beauty becomes animated and refined. It is no longer physical, material, brutal. She escapes from the absolutism of the line; she steps out so to speak from the type in which she was imprisoned and flashes with the light of liberty. She acquires lightness, animation, the spiritual liveliness which the beholder finds in her face, either in fancy or because it is there. She discovers the soul and the secret of modern beauty, —expression. Her depths, her reflexions, her smile come as you gaze at her, her eye speaks. Irony lies at the corner of her mouth and on her half-opened lips. Intelligence passes over her face and transfigures it,—palpitating, trembling, breathing intelligence brings into play all those invisible fibres that transform a face by expression, giving it a thousand shades of caprice, working upon it with the finest modulations, conferring upon it all sorts of delicacies. The intelligence of the eighteenth century models the woman's face upon the masque of the comedy of Marivaux, so mobile, so finely shaded, so delicate and so prettily animated by all the coquetry of the heart, of charm and of taste."

Early in the century the ideal lady was brunette and striking; under Louis the Sixteenth she was blond and appealing. The Louis Quinze lady painted her lips and cheeks, not with the hard conventional crimson of the Regency, but delicately and with character. The Chevalier d'Elbée, who wished to raise a fund to pension the wives and widows of officers, proposed a tax on rouge for the purpose. His pamphlet states that more than 2,000,000 pots were sold annually in France at six francs the pot. Towards the end of the century when the lady became sentimental the use of rouge diminished greatly. She returned to nature, and that there should be no mistake about her intention, she sometimes had herself bled to secure the pale, transparent cheek of naïve sensibility.

Watteau dressed the lady in the famous garment which to this day carries his name, a great robe, almost formless, with short full sleeves, falling behind in a great double pleat or with merely gathered fulness and trailing about the wearer. This robe enabled the lady to reconcile the two opposing motives of woman's dress, conventional stiffness and natural lines. For beneath the robe she wore a corset and the petticoat that was presently to swell into a revival of the farthingale. Thus her body was severely outlined beneath the robe, while the robe itself, loose-fitting, floating, constantly detaching itself from strict relation to the contours of the wearer, made her dress romantic. This robe endured with modifications until the fall of the monarchy. As the inflations of the farthingale proceeded, the skirt of the robe parted in front, revealing the *falbala,* a triangle of highly-ornamented petticoat. Presently the robe itself was pressed into the service of the farthingale and gathered on either side into the paniers which are perhaps the best known mode of the age. Early in the century the lady's hair was dressed low and she wore a little lace cap with strings. Later her coiffure became portentous. The names of Legros and Léonard are less celebrated only than that of John Law. The whole history of the century was reflected in the lady's head-dress which became a rebus. Everyone has read of the *coiffure à la circonstance* which mourned the death of Louis XV with a cypress behind and a cornucopia resting on a sheaf of wheat before; of the *bonnet à la Belle-Poule* which exhibited a frigate under full sail in honour of a naval engagement with the English; of the *coiffure à la Mappemonde,* which displayed on the wearer's head the five divisions of the known globe; and of the *bonnet au Parc Anglais,* with shrubberies and lawns, rivulets, shepherdesses and sheep, and of the *coiffure à l'Inoculation* which represented small-pox by a serpent, medical science by a club, and the result of their encounter by a rising sun and an olive-tree in fruit.

A few years before the Revolution, all this changed. The paniers were let down, the far-thingale was abandoned, high heels were cut off, the hair was dressed meagrely with a garland of flowers, muslin replaced silk, the dress was made simply, *à la Jean Jacques Rousseau, à la Bergere,* or *à la Paysanne.* Under all these disguises the lady remained the same, self-conscious, intelligent, striving to express herself or at any rate to express something. Of all the motives that lead mankind to wear clothes hers was the most artificial. She dressed neither for warmth, nor for decency, nor in the interests of beauty. Her motive was simply that of the actor,—she dressed for her part.

II

THE difference between the status of the lady at Athens in the fifth century before Christ and her status in France in the eighteenth century of our era is so profound that other social changes seem comparatively negligible. The status of property had undergone relatively little change. With some modifications of terminology, labour was exploited as of old. The functions of the gentleman were approximately what they had always been. Adam Smith's analysis of the economic composition of society revealed practically the same constituent elements and motives as Plato's. The lady alone of all classes of society had succeeded in breaking her tabu and, while leaving her economic basis untouched, in altering her social relations in several fundamental directions. She retained what she had originally and added provinces on every side. At Athens she was allowed the dignities belonging to the head of the household on condition of entire fidelity to her husband. In France she even strengthened her position in the house while no longer fulfilling the condition. She had of old been a lady as distinguished from a courtesan; in the eighteenth century the distinction had disappeared except as between amateurs and professionals. Her private security had of old been connected,—indissolubly as men supposed—with her abstinence from public activity; in the later period she strengthened her hand at home by the importance she gained abroad. But since her economic position was unchanged, since men were still officially in control and what she enjoyed was won by favour, it was necessary that all the changes in her position should be wrought by the connivance of men. Her very great ability could not proceed directly to its goal, but must begin by recommending her to men. She was therefore seated in the fork of a perpetual dilemma; to gain her ends, whether in politics or in millinery or in letters, she must cultivate her powers, but how far could she cultivate them without giving offence to men? No one but a Puritan will imagine that to be the mistress of a king or a minister or a savant—to be Madame de Pompadour or Madame de Boufflers or Mlle. de Lespinasse—was a matter simply of *beaux yeux*. Such women and hundreds more of the same type were possessed of talents so great that if they had been men they would have been men of distinction. Being women, they had not only to be agreeable in a positive sense, but they had to draw a veil over what might displease if seen too clearly,—over the unremitting intellectual labour which alone enabled them to achieve their ends. They were permitted to undertake great responsibilities provided they preserved an air of being unfit for them, and to present every other evidence of genius provided they dissembled the capacity to take infinite pains.

The education the lady received in her youth before she took the matter in hand herself was not of a sort to raise the presumption of pedantry against her. The convent was the only school and its graduates could not always read and write. The four younger daughters of Louis XV could not when they were "finished" at Fontevrault. Thirty years later the little girl who became Madame Roland received a favourable impression at the school of the Congregation, which was one of the best of its day. The sister in charge of instruction was an object of jealousy because of her superior attainments which consisted of a beautiful handwriting, skill with the needle, a knowledge of orthography and some acquaintance with history. Thirty-four pupils from six years old to eighteen occupied a single room and were divided into two classes. The ethical side of the children's training was open to criticism as well as the pedagogical. Little penitents were sent alone to pray in the crypt where the dead nuns were buried. A child of five who had committed a theft was sentenced to be hanged. A block and tackle were fixed to the ceiling, the felon was placed in a clothes-basket and hoisted up, while the nuns sang the *De Profundis*. Another child cried "Are you dead?" "Not yet," replied the victim. Thirty years later when one child was the wife of a maréchal of France and the other a duchess, they used smilingly to repeat the formula in greeting each other in society. But some little girls acquired under such discipline the habit of nervous terrors which was lifelong. To balance their severities, the good sisters allowed the most surprising privileges. Many convents received ladies from the world as transient guests and these inmates brought the world with them. Madame de Genlis, shortly after her marriage, sojourned in a convent while her husband was absent on military duty. She enjoyed herself thoroughly. The abbess used to invite men to dinner in her apartment; at the carnival, Madame de Genlis was allowed to give in the convent-parlour two balls a week attended by nuns and school girls; when these amusements were insufficient she would sometimes rise at midnight, run about the corridor in the costume of the devil and wake the nuns in their cells. When she found a sister very sound asleep she would paint her cheeks and affix a *mouche* or two. The little girls were often allowed free access to the lady-boarders and listened with round eyes to their tales of life in the world.

The hygiene of the early eighteenth century was primitive everywhere, and the convent was not a leader in reform. Bathing was discouraged. The children sometimes slept in their clothes, either for fear of the cold or to be able to lie a few minutes longer in the morning. They were required to rise early, and yet they had no food until nine o'clock, although the last meal had been taken at not later than six the night before. There was apparently no ventilation in either school-room or dormitory, and no systematic open-air exercise. The corset was an article of faith, and very careful convents required the pupil to sleep in it lest the good work of the day among her organs be undone at night.

If a little girl were not sent to the convent but educated at home she was not likely to fare very much better. If her parents were thoughtless, she grew up as best she might; if they were thoughtful, they were pretty sure to have a theory of education of which the child was to be the living vindication. No subject was more congenial to the theorists of the eighteenth century; every one had a plan for the regeneration of society, and every one began soundly enough with the training of the child. Stéphanie-Félicité Ducrest de Saint-Aubin, who was later as Madame de Genlis an authority on education, learned to read at the age of five from the teacher of the village school of Saint-Aubin. From her mother's maids she learned a little catechism and plenty of ghost-stories. At the age of seven she had a governess and music-mistress, a girl of sixteen who knew nothing. The curriculum included the catechism, the harpsichord and an abridgment of Buffier's history. After a few days, Buffier was found dull and was replaced by Mademoiselle Scudery's novel of *Clélie*. Now Monsieur de Saint-

Aubin, her father, was a scholar and a student
of natural science. He was devoted to his little girl and might have given her a first-rate
education. But his hobby was to make her a
"femme forte," and the means he adopted was
to teach her to handle spiders and frogs and to
keep pet mice, with a view to putting her on
good terms with creatures so often misunderstood. Her mother was a poet. Her contribution to the child's mental development was to
cause her to learn and act parts in comic opera
and in the tragedies of Voltaire. She was also
dressed in boy's clothes and taught to fence. It
was not until after her marriage that she bravely
and successfully undertook her own education.
Apart from the bizarreries of her experience it
was the general lot. The cultivated women
who organized and dominated a highly intellectual society had no education. Madame du
Deffand learned nothing at her convent; Madame Geoffrin never mastered the art of spelling.
The most obvious inference is somewhat damag-
ing to education. Is not the great mental
energy of these women, their good judgment,
their sound taste, their indefatigable love of
letters, evidence of the advantage enjoyed by
minds unjaded by routine?

III

THE circumstances which worked together to bring the lady to her climax in France in the eighteenth century were of a very much more general character than the education of the individual. The value that we attach to education is part of the democratic theory of life which swept the lady off her feet at the end of her great century. The aristocratic theory of life, which was of necessity hers, has never laid great stress upon education. Scholarship may be a gentleman's hobby, but in a truly aristocratic age no very large number of gentlemen will be educated. The discipline involved in education as we understand it is repugnant to the gentleman's instincts and indeed to some extent destructive of his qualities which should be of an arbitrary and idiosyncratic character. Such instruction as he receives should logically be imparted to him in solitude; nothing is so likely as the pursuit of knowledge in the company of others to widen the gentleman's sympathies, to expose him to unprejudiced competition and to standardise his mind unless it be really original. But all these processes are inimical to his type. Even less is education helpful to the lady. To insist upon educating her is practically to require her to be something other than she has been. Her own demand for education in the nineteenth century was one of the most striking fruits of the democratic movement.

The fundamental occasion of the great efflorescence of the lady under Louis the Fifteenth was the peculiar social temper of the French, finding free play in favourable external conditions, which had been developing ever since the days of Louis the Eleventh. The lady's acknowledged importance as a factor in civilised social life is plainly noted in the tales and by-play of the Heptameron. If her progress was interrupted, the interruption was due to the relapse into barbarism known as the wars of religion. These once over, the lady's future was assured; she had but to take her own. Even Louis the Fourteenth could not suppress her. The French sense of solidarity made her essential to the social scheme, and the century which in England developed the coffee-house and Dr. Johnson developed in France the salon.

The art of the *salonière* is in its nature unsusceptible of comparative criticism, like that of the actress. Just as we have to accept our grandfathers' decision in regard to the genius of Rachel, so we must infer what we may from the enthusiasm of her contemporaries concerning the charm of Mademoiselle de Lespinasse.

It is a somewhat striking fact that the portraits of the most famous *salonières* show them—even through the good-will of the artist—as plain. Madame Geoffrin's portentous ugliness, the irregularity of Mademoiselle de Lespinasse, the *chinoiserie* of Madame de Tencin, the angular features of Madame du Deffand, are an enduring proof of their power.   But it would be a bold woman who should argue from their example that to be plain and to have no education are in themselves the basis of social success.

One result of the lady's lack of education was her restriction to the field of action which is always most congenial and easiest to her, the field of personal influence. She had plenty of ideas but she could not express them impersonally.

The men of the eighteenth century were throwing off with amazing facility works of novel content and imperishable form; they were affecting each other and the world at large in an almost unexampled way by pure reason made digestible by the vehicle of style. Rousseau, for instance, the dominating influence of his time, had the least possible capacity for dealing personally with the world. His impassioned vanity, his exaggerations, his injustice, his credulities and misfortunes, are such as we think of as belonging in general to the temperament of women. In fact, it will be seen that he differed from the typical lady of his day almost as much in temperament as in the power of sustained production. It is true that after his day the lady tended somewhat to reproduce his type and under his influence to become romantic. But the ladies who were his contemporaries had precisely and for good reasons the personal qualities that he lacked. Their vanity was without passion, for it was without illusions. The simplicity, the need of approbation, the naïve sensibility that made him so gullible were incompatible with the lady's experience of life. His genius could play only in a world of illusions, hers only in the cold white light of psychological analysis. A man whose function was merely to write great books could do so with his eyes closed; the lady whose success in life was to consist in exploiting him was compelled to keep hers open. Her first business was to understand herself, her second to understand her world. Nothing is more surprising to the Anglo-Saxon, who believes in unpremeditated art, than the fact that beauty is not necessary to make a Frenchwoman seductive. The power of mind when applied to the science of being agreeable is something of which he has very little conception. His

women have an *amour propre* which forbids
them to try to please. The admiration they
excite without trying is the only kind they value.
Both man and woman are almost inaccessible to
the motive of which Montesquieu says: *"Ce
désir général de plaire produit la galanterie,
qui n'est point l'amour, mais le délicat, mais
le leger, mais le perpétuel mensonge de
l'amour."*

The French lady of the eighteenth century
on the other hand aimed to please as whole-
heartedly as a grocer aims to sell cabbages.
Her enthusiasm often carried her to the length
of pleasing her husband. Her intimate man-
friends she pleased without too much trouble,
and she was very careful to please her woman-
friends as well. In the political world the
women (Montesquieu says) all had relations with
each other and formed a sort of republic, a
state within the state, the members of which
were always active in mutual good offices. But
the lady counted these steps as but preliminary;
she was a failure unless she pleased all her
world. It is a somewhat discouraging fact
that if she is to give a great deal of pleasure,
the lady must not in general be impetuously
affectionate. She must not care for people to
the extent of failing to understand them or to
act on her understanding. A tough, unenthus-

iastic good-nature, like that of Madame Geoffrin is an excellent basis for her activities.
Madame Geoffrin was endlessly kind to many
people; but her most famous saying, which
Count de Schomberg called sublime, shows
other qualities. She offered thirty thousand
francs to Rulhière to destroy or even to ex-
purgate his scandalous manuscript on Russia.
Rulhière turned upon her with indignation at
the idea that a historian could be bribed to suppress the truth as he saw it. "Well," said
Madame Geoffrin, "how much more do you
want?" An invincible good sense was the companion of the essential good humour, and between them they left little reason for folly.
The lady could give sound advice on any practical subject; one counselled a young man "to
make friends among women rather than among
men, for through the women you can manage
the men. Also some men are too dissipated and
the rest are too much preoccupied with their
own affairs to attend to yours, but the women will
give real thought to them if only because they
have nothing else to do. But when you have
singled out the women who can be useful to
you, take care you don't make love to them."
Another listened to the comedy of a young
friend, and made this comment for his benefit:
"At your age it is possible to write good verses

but not a good comedy; that is the product not only of talent but of experience. You have studied the drama, but, luckily for you, you have not yet had time to study the world. Portraits cannot be painted without models. Frequent society where the ordinary man sees nothing but faces, the man of talent discovers physiognomies. And do not imagine that you must live in the great world to know it; look about you and you will perceive that it contains the vices and follies of all classes. At Paris above all the stupidities and perversities of the great are rapidly reproduced in lower circles, and perhaps it is even better for the comic author to study them there because they are there shown more artlessly and unrelieved. In every age manners have a character of their own which must be seized. Do you know what is the most distinguished trait of our manners to-day?" The young man suggested that it was gallantry. "No," said his monitress, "it is vanity."

The ladies of the court of Francis the First delighted in a sort of erotic mysticism that included both sacred and profane love. Love and religion were interwoven in an emotion not too clearly analysed. The ladies of the eighteenth century had no illusions about either, and one of them expressed thus her notion of the re-

lation between them. "You must never tell
your lover that you do not believe in God. As
to your husband, it doesn't matter. But with
a lover you must always keep a retreat open,
and a religious scruple can end a love-affair at
once."

To suppose that the life of the *salonière* consisted in giving pleasant parties is to mistake the
flower for the root and the branch. The force
of these strong and gifted ladies showed itself
everywhere where personal influence can count,
that is throughout the field of social relations.
The ablest of all had a controlling voice in the
affairs of the state, instructed ambassadors, determined the fate of ministers. The very des-
patches of the time show a feminine style and
abound in *"mots de ruelle."* Cardinal de Tencin and the Duke de Choiseul expressed the
wills of Madame de Tencin and the Duchess de
Gramont. Madame de Langeac could command *lettres de cachet,* Mademoiselle Renard
could create general officers, Mademoiselle
Guimard could distribute benefices. The sur-
est way into the Academy was through a lady's
recommendation; the success of a play, a poem,
a picture, a philosophy, depended upon her.
The lady is the sturdy oak, the man of genius
the clinging vine; Madame de Luxembourg
protects Rousseau, Madame de Richelieu pro-

tects Voltaire; Madame de Choiseul protects the
Abbé Barthelemy; Mademoiselle de Lespinasse
protects de Guibert.

It was not until the middle of the century
that the diffused feminism of the age crystal-
lised in the salon. The great ladies of the
Regency chose other modes of activity and the
lesser ladies were still oppressed by the tradition of Versailles with its doctrine of social cen-
tralisation. A work called *Reflexion nou-
velles sur les Femmes, par une Dame de la
Cour,* published in 1727, complains of the lack
of reasonable intercourse and looks back with
regret to the days of the Hôtel de Rambôuillet
and its Platonic conversations. Slowly as the
century advanced a lady ventured here and there
to institute a weekly supper-party. One by one
the houses were built that were to make private
entertainments possible. In exactly the middle
of the century the lady who had formerly been
Madame de Boufflers and had recently become
the Maréchale de Luxembourg founded the
salon which while remaining for fifty years the
most famous of its class furnished inspiration
for the opening of many more. The Maréchale
gave regularly two suppers a week; but these
were the least of her cares. It was plain to her
that she must have a man of acknowledged
parts as her chief attraction and she fixed upon

the Comte de Bissy as the man. The steps by which she secured the count will serve as well as another example to illustrate the thoroughness of the lady's methods. In the first place, she persuaded her friend the Duchess de la Vallière to dismiss an old admirer and instal de Bissy in his place. But unwilling to rely on a sentimental claim alone, she contrived through the influence of Madame de Pompadour to have de Bissy admitted to the Academy. In return for these various values received, the count became the official wit of the Maréchale's salon.

It was in that one house as much as anywhere that the theory and practice of good society were brought to perfection, under the formative influence of the lady. The Goncourts in their enthusiasm declare that the lady furnished a glimpse of heaven to a godless age: *"la femme arrive à être pour le dix-huitième siecle, non-seulement le dieu de bonheur, du plaisir, de l'amour, mais l'être poétique, l'être sacré par excellence, le but de toute élévation morale, l'idéal humain incarné dans un sexe de l'humanité."* To admit these statements is to accept the Frenchman's view of life, to believe that agreeable social relations are the noblest thing our race has achieved, and that the conception of manners formulated in the salon, and modified but not destroyed by the Revolution, remains the basis of civilised existence. This view of life, however little accepted by peoples of Teutonic blood, is one to which the lady everywhere secretly or openly, unconsciously or even despite herself, inclines. Not only she, but women in general, are best off in a highly artificial society. We have come to realise that the equality of opportunity which was the desideratum of the early friends of woman's industrial advancement is not enough. The working-woman must have a special situation created for her if society is to get the utmost from her that she can do. In unrestricted competition with men she comes to grief and the race is injured. In primitive social conditions therefore she is bound to go to the wall. Hence the working-woman as well as the lady has an instinct that favours a conventional as opposed to a natural social situation. Their interests are it is true essentially opposed, but they agree in shrinking from the naïve law of force. The lady is the product of man's earliest æsthetic desires, and it is her business in every way to foster these. It is only among peoples who easily and naturally rise to the conception of life as an art that she is able to attain her full growth, and her classic claim to measure the civilisation of a nation by the degree of perfection in which it produces the lady is to this extent and in this sense valid.

The lady of the salon formulated this art of life in a very high spirit and called it *"politesse."* Its principles were historically derived from those which Marie de Champagne and her friends had dictated to the world through the literature of courteous love; but these had been profoundly modified. The knight was gone, and the lady was emancipated. In the social struggle she fought with the same weapons and the same chance of success as her lord. Instead, therefore, of two codes of conduct for the sexes with love as the only common ground, *politesse* was as nearly as possible the same for both sexes. The primary division of society, one may say, was not into male and female, but into polite and rude. Of this distinction, the lady was absolute judge; the salon was the assembly of the elect and without there was weeping and gnashing of teeth. The spectacle of French *politesse* in full swing had elements both of fascination and of terror for the English mind. It is interesting to watch its reaction upon for instance Horace Walpole, who at home so often felt himself but an indifferent Englishman. Like all other arts, the art of life made a strong appeal to Walpole, but he could stand only a limited amount of it. His individualism was fretted by the constant implication of reference to an absolute standard, and, good Whig though he was, he was too strongly aristocratic by temperament to be at home in the most aristocratic society in the world. Though a kindly man and a gentleman he reserved the right as an Englishman of distinction to be rude if he liked. And it shocked him, whom so little could shock, to hear the propositions of philosophy bandied about as table-talk. He dearly loved to talk to ladies but not on serious topics, even if they were treated flippantly. His relation with Madame du Deffand is one of the drollest as well as one of the most touching of international episodes. Her powers and charms were of the sort to be irresistible to him; he felt as profoundly as a Frenchman could do the value of her friendly intercourse as a criticism of life. But he never mastered the feeling that as an Englishman he was making a fool of himself. Who in England could understand his attachment for an old woman? His friends would reason that either he was in love with her or he was not, and that if anything could be more ridiculous than a love affair with an old woman, it was a strong and abiding interest in a woman with whom one was not in love. *Politesse* was not so thoroughly understood by his countrymen

as to make the matter intelligible to them. One
of the things indeed that Walpole was forever
commenting on in French society was its acceptance of women no longer young. The lady's
riper age is generally a very difficult question.
When she is really old the matter is comparatively simple; if circumstances put power in her
hands she can be a magnificent and formidable
phenomenon. If nature has been kind to her
physically she can assume the frail and exquisite
grace of a china mantle-ornament. If she is
neither powerful nor lovely she must occupy
herself with giving as little trouble as possible.
These various courses are practically dictated
to her by circumstances. But the years of
transition present a real problem, and in the
solution the lady of the salon showed her genius.
She had never allowed mere physical beauty to
have things all its own way, as it has always
had them in England. In suffering plain
women gladly, the most lovely kept open her
own retreat; a society accustomed to other than
bodily charms would not notice their decay.
The lady never achieved a more striking *tour de
force* than in her triumph over the primitive
instinct of man in favour of change and youth.
In the eighteenth century she kept her lovers
long;—no picture of the time is complete without an ancient marquise and an ancient count,

united by tender recollections,—and she kept society as long as she lived. As a sheer triumph of spirit over flesh, she might well regard her work as the highest point in the civilisation she was ever striving to impose upon man.

The admirers of *politesse* are wont to remind us that it furnished in a godless age an excellent imitation of most of the Christian virtues. If you were bent on hurting your neighbour's feelings, *politesse* compelled you to do so in the most considerate way. If you were intent on outshining your dearest friend as a hostess, you could do so only by exhibiting more completely than she the power of self-effacement which would enable the egotism of your guests to expand and flower. If you wished to convict a rival of vulgarity you must outdo him in magnanimity. Physical and moral courage were matters of course. To lose your temper was as gross a social fault as to drink from your finger-bowl. In England the higher your rank, the more people you might scold. In France as you ascended the social scale your possibilities of abuse became more and more confined, and the most distinguished never allowed themselves to be excited at all. The root of all these virtues was a self-esteem which has always fascinated even those of mankind who are temperamentally unfit to entertain it. It is the final expression of man's protest against nature and against fate. It is the motive that upheld Prometheus. More timid spirits watch its manifestations with the fearful joy entertained by little boys when a big boy defies the schoolmaster. It does in the moral world what art does in its own,—opposes the will and judgment of man to the crudity and incoherence of the natural order. It satisfies one of the most deeply seated of human instincts, the instinct to impose form on confusion. The immortal charm of the old régime is witness to the sense of relief with which the restless modern spirit sees the whole of life relentlessly based on a principle, right or wrong, for which its entertainers are prepared to undergo the final disaster. The fate of an early Christian virgin and martyr makes a touching story, but we understand that her reward was so immediately before her eyes that the intermediate step looked short to her and therefore may to us. It is a very different and more tonic appeal, an appeal that throws us back upon whatever there be of stoicism and self-reliance in our own breasts, that is made to us when the lady of the salon affixes her last *mouche* and makes her toilette for the guillotine.

THE LADY OF THE BLUE STOCKINGS

"The calamities of an unhappy marriage are so much greater than can befal a single person, that the unmarried woman may find abundant argument to be contented with her condition."
MRS. CHAPONE, *On the Improvement of the Mind.*

M. GASTON PARIS tells us that we are to infer from Geoffrey of Monmouth's account of the court of Arthur that the England of Henry the Second was the home of manners. Prowess and courtesy were there inseparable and life became polite. With the exception of this purely exotic and imported exhibition of the art of life, it cannot be said that English history reveals any noticeable practice of politeness except for a brief time and under special conditions in the eighteenth century, when it was again imposed from abroad by the overwhelming genius of the neighbour nation. Politeness is not the natural expression of Teutonic social instincts because it implies at one remove what the Teuton prefers to express directly. It is the natural expression of the social instincts of people of lively wits who actually prefer to think of two things at once. It makes life a perpetual game of whist instead of a game of cricket. An exact analogy to the Teutonic theory of social intercourse is to be found in Herbert Spencer's theory of literary style. The aim of the written word, according to his well-known exposition, is to convey the writer's meaning to the reader with the least possible draught on the attention of the latter; nothing must distract him, no irrelevancies must waste his nervous force, the different parts of speech must be fed to him in mathematical relation to his needs, as though he were a model-baby or a type-setting machine. The result of this theory as practised by the expounder of it is that the active-minded reader has not enough to think about to keep him busy. Mere words and especially long Latin ones cannot be presented with sufficient rapidity by the eye to keep the brain supplied. The reader of Herbert Spencer is practically driven to do something else at the same time, to pat a dog or to listen to a conversation in the next room, in order to keep his faculties occupied. The English-speaking peoples have in general been nurtured on so generous a diet of abounding and satisfying literary style, that they readily perceive the defect in Spencer's practice, however much his theory may strike them as rational; but they often find it hard to realise that what they need in literature on pain of feeling

empty, other peoples more used to purely intellectual diversions need throughout the social
relations. To state the matter in the simplest
terms, there are two ways of proving your
superiority if a man in a crowd speaks rudely
to you; one is to knock him down and the other
is not to. The first method has several advantages; it is unambiguous and it is intelligible to
all. The second method is ambiguous; it may
as easily mean that you are afraid as that you
are superior, and it is intelligible only to those
who understand the rules of the game. The
first method, it need hardly be said, is felt, whatever else it may be, to be "English." The second method, though freely practised by sophisticated Englishmen, is an acquisition. It substitutes for the demonstrable superiority of the
biceps a superiority which rests on abstract
consideration, and it therefore compels thought.
The common consent of civilisation has imposed
certain limits on the Teutonic theory of social
intercourse, so that although most so-called
Anglo-Saxons are still conscious of the instinct
to hit out, many of them have it more or less
under control. They are as far as ever, however, from accepting the general theory that life
is more amusing if many of its acts mean two
things at once. Good manners are for them a
set of rules, not a principle of spontaneous ac-

tion. They still cherish the theory that a good
measure of a man's social importance is the
number of people to whom he may with im-
punity be rude. Nothing is more striking to an
outlander who watches an Englishman on his
way up in the world than to note from year to
year the added number of minutes that he ventures to keep people waiting. Of course, what
the Englishman relies on to temper the dynamic
way of conducting social relations is the excellence of his heart. He thinks of himself as
a kindly giant. What can any society have better in the way of atmosphere than "fair play?"
In his eyes, it may even be said, uniform good
manners are an admission on the part of the
owner that he is not perfectly sure of his position in society. Moreover, they actually limit
the field of action of a naturally generous
temper. Where all are polite, how is the kindly
man to make himself known? He is no better
than any one else and might as well not be kindly
at all. One of the reasons for the chronic passing of the lie between the French and the English is their lack of sympathy on this question.
The Englishman argues that to exhibit habitu-
ally a suavity beyond what human nature is capable of entertaining is dishonest. The Frenchman raises an eyebrow at the notion of an excellence of heart which is apparently most natu-

rally expressed by an easy disregard of the feelings of others.

This matter which forms so curious a spectacle for the impartial outsider is one of profound importance for the lady. The strength of her position waxes and wanes with the shifting importance of manners. When they reach their climax, as in the eighteenth century in France, so does she. As she gains influence she uses it to make manners prevail, but she cannot of herself originate an atmosphere congenial to them. The proposition is generally stated in the other sense, but it seems truer to say that manners make the lady than that the lady makes manners. Such at any rate is the conclusion to be drawn from a vigorous effort made by certain ladies of England, taking advantage of a temporary national enthusiasm for manners, to break through the social limitations of their sex and induce men to accept their social value as the same as that of the ladies of France.

It was to the ladies of France that the ladies of England naturally looked for lessons in the social art. A little work translated from the French and called *The Art of Being Easy at all Times and in all Places, written chiefly for the use of a Lady of Quality,* was a popular manual in many English homes. Good Mrs. Chapone, in writing to her niece those wonderful *Letters on the Improvement of the Mind,* which were the gospel of the new sect, was swift to admit that the young lady will probably realise that politeness—"this delightful qualification, so universally admired and respected but so rarely possessed in any eminent degree,"—is not among her natural endowments. It belongs by nature only to very quick-witted people. "To be perfectly polite," says Mrs. Chapone, "one must have great presence of mind, with a delicate and quick sense of propriety; or in other words one should be able to form an instantaneous judgment of what is fittest to be said or done, on every occasion as it offers. I have known one or two persons who seemed to owe this advantage to nature only, and to have the peculiar happiness of being born as it were with another sense, by which they had an immediate perception, of what was proper and improper, in cases absolutely new to them; but this is the lot of very few; in general propriety of behaviour must be the fruit of instruction, of observation and reasoning; and is to be cultivated and improved like any other branch of knowledge or virtue." Without counting, then, on any great natural aptitude, the English lady set to work with grammar and dictionary to learn to be easy at all times and in all places.

But though manners were to be the foundation of the new movement, the lady was not to depend upon their charm alone. Her conversation was to have a solid value; it should be possible for ladies to converse together to their entertainment and profit without the uplift of men's presence. There was a respectable if apologetic tradition in England in the seventeenth century that women were as susceptible of education as men. Men's parts being cultivated and refined by learning and the arts are like an enclosed piece of common, (said Dr. Allestree in *The Ladies Calling*) which by industry and husbandry becomes a different thing from the rest, but the natural turf owned no such inequality. Queen Elizabeth and Lady Jane Grey were doubtless largely responsible for the gentility allowed to learning in ladies, though it was more often explicitly attributed to Sappho and Cornelia, who were even more undeniably acquainted respectively with Greek and Latin. Towards the end of the seventeenth century a work was published by a Mrs. Makin with the title *An Essay to revive the Ancient Education of Gentlewomen in Religion, Manners, Arts and Tongues: With an Answer to the Objections against this way of Education.* As the title implies, the argument rests on the assumption that at some time past women were the recipients of a strenuous and liberal education. The reader's interest is stimulated to enquire whether the author has in mind the ladies of the twelfth century who patronised the literature of courteous love, or the learned nuns of centuries before the twelfth. It turns out, however, that her reference is more remote and the education she proposes to revive is that bestowed upon the Sibyls. Her historical summary leaps in fact from ancient Rome to Lady Jane Grey and the "present Duchess of Newcastle." After protesting against "the barbarous custom to breed women low," and proposing a better course, Mrs. Makin adds a postscript to her essay: "If any enquire where this education may be performed, such may be informed that a school is lately erected for Gentlewomen at Tottenham High Cross, within four miles of London, on the road to Ware, where Mrs. Makin is governess, who was formerly tutoress to the Princess Elizabeth, daughter to King Charles the First." According to the prospectus of Mrs. Makin's school, half the time was to be spent in dancing, music, singing, writing and keeping accounts. "The other half to be employed in gaining the Latin and French tongues; and those that please may learn Greek and Hebrew, the Italian and Spanish: in all which this Gentlewoman hath a competent knowledge.

"Gentlewomen of eight or nine years old that can read well may be instructed in a year or two (according to their parts) in the Latin and French tongues.

"Repositories also for Visibles shall be prepared: by which, from beholding the things, Gentlewomen may learn the Names, Natures, Values and Use of Herbs, Shrubs, Trees, Mineral-pieces, Metals and Stones.

"Those that please may learn Limning, Preserving, Pastry and Cookery.

"Those that will allow longer time may attain some general knowledge in Astronomy, Geography, but especially in Arithmetic and History."

The reader cannot but recall the programme with which, as Miss Wirt assured Mr. Snob, she and her young charges managed to "pass the days at the Evergreens not unpleasantly."

Mrs. Makin's school was successful, gave rise to imitators and helped to fortify the tradition of the learned gentlewoman. Here was educated Elizabeth Middleton, the mother of Mrs. Edmund Montagu, the chief of the Blue-Stockings, who may thus fairly be considered the product at one remove of Mrs. Makin's system. But apart from this concrete instance of its effect, it is fair to take it as a point of departure because nothing could so well illustrate the fundamental difference between the methods of the English lady and those of her model, the lady of France. The French lady made herself a highly cultivated person. The knowledge of letters and history possessed by such a woman as Madame du Deffand is something that cannot be matched in England at all as far as the records go; but she had no idea of posing as the possessor of scholarship. She knew very well that no greater handicap can be attached to the power of woman to please than the reputation, whether well-founded or not, of possessing exact information. It is true that an honest man may be successful under democratic institutions, and in the same sense a learned woman may be successful in society; but in each case much more ability is required than if the qualification did not exist. In the eighteenth century there was no machinery in either France or England for turning out really learned women. Mrs. Makin's establishment could hardly do for girls what Oxford was doing for their brothers; the French lady was saved by her discretion and by her sense of humour from any attempt to compete with men. Appreciation and suggestion were her weapons. She could not, it is true, know too much for their skilful exercise, but she made no pretensions. She achieved results and left others to comment on them. She began with the practice of social success, leaving posterity to derive the theory from her *chefs-d'œuvre,* as it does in the case of the sculpture of the Greeks. But the English lady began by a somewhat defiant announcement of her pretensions. It may easily have seemed to her that it was safer in view of the unpromising state of English society, which certainly did not demand the salon, to pursue learning for its own sake in order to have something to show for her exertions in case the social result was meagre. The difference is a profound one; it is connected with the sturdy preference of the Englishwoman for standing on her own feet, and both are part of the individualism of her race which, uncongenial to an age of manners, blossomed out in the nineteenth century in a variety of striking types under conditions that left the French lady nowhere. The methods that led to success when pursued by Florence Nightingale and Octavia Hill were inapplicable to the problem and conditions of the eighteenth century. It was the avowed intention of the ladies who became know as the Blue-Stockings to supplant card-playing by conversation; but they approached card-playing as though it were a gun-shot wound or a congested tenement district.

Neither right reason nor acts of Parliament could effect the reform they had in view. Nothing could do it but charm, and the measure of charm they were able to exert was of a sort to attract only those who were of their way of thinking already.

There was one aspect of life in England in the eighteenth century that was favourable to the ambitious lady. This aspect was the result of the unexampled personality of politics. The Hanoverian monarchs systematised a feminism at court which, though naïve and coarse, in comparison with the analogous phenomenon in France, was something to be taken into account by ministers. The career of Lord Hervey, who was selected by Sir Robert Walpole for the explicit purpose of managing the queen, is a salient case by which to estimate the shift of things since that day. Walpole was a statesman of a very high order, yet among the objects of his solicitude the proper manipulation of the queen ranked with the excise and questions of war or peace. The politics of the generations succeeding his as reflected in the letters of his son were full of the same element of personal influence, often feminine. Here was an opening for the sort of activity in which the English lady has always excelled, and by virtue of which she may be said to have developed a type of her own, surviving to the present day. The English-woman of rank and fortune, trained from the cradle as if for the profession of diplomacy, in the use of foreign tongues and the discussion of the questions of the day, discreet, sensible, and full of responsibility, contrives to make the best of her national characteristics. She does not trade on her personal charm, being far removed from the necessity to do so, and in the interest of the greater game, she often forgets the question of her own vanity. The lady of the eighteenth century had not yet reached this stage; it was not yet permitted her to be thoroughly businesslike. The age and the tradition of her class still required a certain amount of folly to cloak her seriousness. She was generally of a different stamp altogether from the learned lady. There occurred, however, in the first half of the century a combination of shrewd ability for the personal sort of politics, of strong-minded folly and of the penchant for learning which furnished an instructive study of all these qualities. This combination was Lady Mary Pierrepont, better known as Lady Mary Wortley Montagu. "When I was young," she said in later life, "I was a great admirer of Ovid's *Metamorphoses,* and that was one of the chief reasons that set me upon the thoughts of stealing the Latin language. Mr. Wortley was the only person to whom I communicated my design, and he encouraged me in it. I used to study five or six hours a day for two years in my father's library; and so got that language whilst everybody else thought I was reading nothing but novels and romances." The extraordinary run-away match between a dull, methodical young gentleman and a vivacious young lady, where the misgivings were all on his side and the impetuosity all on hers, the gradual collapse of the interest in Ovid and indeed of all common ground, and the final separation are all good comedy. But the real interest in her case, based on the evidence of her voluminous letters, lies in her great ability, thwarted and wasted, but unmistakable. Having incurred the enmity of Pope and the dislike of Horace Walpole, her chief reporters, Lady Mary has come down to us as the dissipated shrew of the one and as the eccentric untidy old woman of the other. But she was for twenty-five years one of the beauties and wits of London, giving and taking the best that the society of her time afforded. Her letters show the keenness with which a clever woman could read the personal side of public affairs. There was a whole field of politics in which great matters were rooted, and which could still be cultivated by persons, both men and women, who had no pretensions to statesmanship or to a knowledge of political economy. How much more favourable this condition of things was to the lady's participation in politics than the present prevalence of business methods requiring the laborious mastery of detail, hardly needs to be pointed out. It was the most stimulating possibility her time had for her. Apart from this possibility, restricted in the nature of things to a few persons exceptionally placed in the world, society could offer hardly any triumphs to the lady save a year or two of notoriety as a reigning toast. The public against which the Blue-Stockings organised their attempt was as difficult as participants in a forlorn hope could desire.

If we look into the eighteenth century in England through two or three of the very differently placed windows opened for us by contemporary accounts, we find the social landscape, however varied, agreeing in one marked contrast to the French. Neither Horace Walpole nor Dr. Johnson wanted ladies' society as it was understood in France. Horace Walpole went frequently to Paris; the best friend of his middle life was an old French lady; he had at home an almost absurd air of French urbanity and the highly polished exterior which is generally deprecated as un-English. But he was not for nothing a connoisseur. He could put up with culture in a French lady; her views of life and letters he found undeniably valuable as well as delightful. But he could not put up with what the English lady presented to him under that name. The political English lady he suffered gladly, Lady Hervey or, on a different plane, Lady Ossory. But when Mrs. Miller established her poetic vase at Batheaston, his joy was of the sort that springs from the sense of humour. "Mrs. Miller," says he, "is returned a beauty, a genius, a Sappho, a tenth Muse, as romantic as Mademoiselle de Scuderi, and as sophisticated as Mrs. Vesey. They have introduced bouts-rimés as a new discovery. They hold a Parnassus fair every Thursday, give out rhymes and themes, and all the flux and quality of Bath contend for the prizes. A Roman vase, decked with pink ribbons and myrtle, receives the poetry, which is drawn out every festival. Six judges of these Olympic games retire and select the brightest compositions, which the respective successful acknowledge, kneel to Mrs. Calliope, kiss her fair hand and are crowned by it with myrtle, with—I don't know what. You may think this a fiction or exaggeration. Be dumb, un-

believers! The collection is printed, published,
—yes, on my faith! there are bouts-rimés on a
buttered muffin by her Grace the Duchess of
Northumberland, receipts to make them by
Corydon the Venerable, alias George Pitt;
others, very pretty, by Lord Palmerston . . .
many by Mrs. Miller herself, that have no fault
but wanting metre."

Dr. Johnson who, as far as the evidence
goes, had seen none of the contents of the
famous vase, dealt with it *à priori* in his
favourite manner. "Bouts-rimés," said he, "is
a mere conceit, and an old conceit now; I wonder how many people were persuaded to write
in that manner for this lady?" I named a
gentleman of his acquaintance who wrote for
the vase. *Johnson.* "He was a blockhead for
his pains." *Boswell.* "The Duchess of Northumberland wrote." *Johnson.* "Sir, the Duchess of Northumberland may do what she
pleases: nobody will say anything to a lady of
her high rank. But I should be apt to throw
——'s verses in his face."

Both Walpole and Johnson preferred conversation to cards, or in fact to any other occupation whatever, but neither cared to talk
seriously to women. Each was the centre of
such a group as in France would have been
gathered about a lady. Other men served as

similar nuclei. Dr. Burney and Sir Joshua Reynolds were really dangerous rivals to the quadrille-table. But a party of men and women was a mechanical mixture, tending constantly to resolve itself into its elements. Mrs. Carter describes such a party. "As if the two sexes had been in a state of war, the gentlemen ranged themselves on one side of the room, where they talked their own talk, and left us poor ladies to twirl our shuttles and amuse each other by conversing as we could. By what little I could hear, our opposites were discoursing on the old English poets, and this subject did not seem so much beyond a female capacity, but that we might have been indulged with a share in it."

If so little encouragement was held out to the lady by the avowedly intellectual society of her time, she had even less prospect of success among the more commonplace. We see the eighteenth century in England a little too exclusively through the medium of the wits. The tincture of French manners introduced by the cosmopolitan part of society has served to give the time in the retrospect a general air of distinction and urbanity. To correct this notion, it is necessary only to read a novel written by a young lady in good society, which was at once acclaimed by her contemporaries as a piece of convincing realism. It was the truth of *Evelina* that carried its readers by storm, and we may accept it, since they did, as a faithful picture of the life of the times. But the life it pictures is one of an almost incredible crudity. The extraordinary carelessness of Evelina's various chaperons which allowed her to fall into one equivocal situation after another is rendered doubly culpable by the character of the society to which she was exposed. Mr. Lovel's immunity from chastisement and Sir Clement Willoughby's unquestioned position in the world are phenomena much more startling than the vulgarity of the shopkeeping Branghtons. What an odd conception of social responsibility must have enabled Mr. Villars, while deploring his ward's misadventures, to tolerate her absence from him for the sake of her "prospects" from her grandmother! One would think that the lightest of Evelina's mortifications would have brought the old gentleman up to town by the next coach. The young lady's own contributory negligence is not the least noteworthy moral phenomenon. But the really striking inference from the facts presented is the universal prevalence of bad manners. Madame Duval of course exists merely for the sake of hers, but what is there to choose between the vocabulary and the regard

for others of the ex-barmaid and of Captain
Mirvan, the gallant officer, the man of family,
and the husband of the most delicate-minded of
her sex? Captain Mirvan with the connivance
of Sir Clement Willoughby plans a practical
joke on Madame Duval, who is at the time an
inmate of his own house. She is decoyed
abroad by a false rumour of the danger of a
friend; her carriage is waylaid by imitation
highwaymen; she is dragged forcibly along the
road with many bumps and shakes and left in
a ditch with her feet tied together. This little
pleasantry is comparable with Tony Lumpkin's
jest of jolting his mother and another lady to a
jelly and finally depositing them in a horse-
pond. Both Goldsmith and Miss Burney delighted their audience with these feats. "How
true and how delightful" said contemporary
criticism. When Evelina's fortunes begin to
mend and she is moving in the best society, she
does not encounter greater tenderness of heart.
Apart from the insolence of the great—for in
England *noblesse permet* rather than *oblige*—
the brutal scene in which Lord Merton and
Mr. Coverly settle their wager by setting two
old women to run a foot race fairly raises the
gorge. When we turn from such pastimes to
the doings of Mrs. Miller and her friends, the

Roman vase with its pink ribbons appears as the symbol of humanity and civilisation.

The reason why the ladies who strove to soften the manners of their age were called "bluestockings" is still so far shrouded in obscurity as to be a promising subject for a doctoral dissertation. But they themselves had no doubts on the subject; they did not derive their name from the *calze turchine* of the Venetian Renaissance, or from any French mode. Madame d'Arblay gives an explicit derivation which is corroborated by Boswell. "To begin," says she, "with what still is famous in the annals of conversation, the Bas Bleu Societies. The first of these was then in the meridian of its lustre, but had been instituted many years previously at Bath. It owed its name to an apology made by Mr. Stillingfleet in declining to accept an invitation to a literary meeting at Mrs. Vesey's, from not being, he said, in the habit of displaying a proper equipment for an evening assembly. 'Pho, Pho,' cried she, with her well-known yet always original simplicity, while she looked inquisitively at him and his accoutrements: 'don't mind dress! Come in your blue stockings!' With which words, humorously repeating them as he entered the apartment of the chosen coterie, Mr. Stillingfleet claimed permission for appearing, according to order. And these words ever after were fixed in playful stigma upon Mrs. Vesey's associations." A correspondent of Mrs. Montagu's writes her that a common acquaintance "swears he will make out some story of you and Stillingfleet before you are much older; you shall not keep blue stockings at Sandleford for nothing." Mrs. Montagu herself writes of Stillingfleet "I assure you, our old philosopher is so much a man of pleasure, he has left off his old friends and his blue stockings and is at operas and other gay assemblies every night." It is to be hoped that the soul of Mr. Stillingfleet derives from the immortality thrust upon him by this derivation a degree of pleasure compensatory for some of the ill-luck of his life. He was the disinherited grandson of the Bishop of Worcester; he drank the cup of mortification as a subsizar at Cambridge; and his ladylove jilted him after a ten years' courtship. His lifelong poverty which as he said was "a specific for some passions," inspired him with a gentle pessimism which gave him a flavour. He readily became the mild wit of the ladies' parties, standing in the same ratio to d'Alembert as Mrs. Vesey to Mademoiselle de Lespinasse. His poem on the *Art of Conversation* deals chiefly like the Decalogue in prohibitions.

Mrs. Vesey and Mrs. Montagu were the chiefs of the Blue-Stockings, and, differing widely in temperament and method, agreed only in aim. They were expositors of two different theories of the Evening Party. Mrs. Montagu was for organisation; she arranged her guests in a semi-circle, after the method of the Duchess of Urbino and Madonna Emilia in the sixteenth century. "The lady of the castle," says Madame d'Arblay, "commonly placed herself at the upper end of the room, near the commencement of the curve, so as to be courteously visible to all her guests; having the person of highest rank or consequence properly on one side, and the person most eminent for talents sagaciously on the other; or as near to her chair and her converse as her favouring eye and a complacent bow of the head could invite him to that distinction." There seems to be no doubt that in Mrs. Montagu's mind the duties of the hostess closely resembled those of the schoolmistress. It was she who suggested the topic, controlled the discussion, called upon this guest or that for an expression of opinion, and finally summed up with the dogmatic finality of the eighteenth century. If she was sometimes a little afraid of her class so that "her liveliest sallies had a something of anxiety rather than of hilarity—till their success was ascertained by applause," this was but natural seeing that such persons as Horace Walpole and Dr. Burney were among the pupils.

Mrs. Vesey on the other hand was an advocate of *laissez faire*. Her fears were so great of "the horror," as it was styled, "of a circle," from the ceremony and awe which it produced, that she pushed all the small sofas as well as chairs pell-mell about the apartments so as not to leave even a zig-zag path of communication free from impediment. Mrs. Vesey's freedom from a didactic aim was, however, but a negative virtue; her friends liked her but it does not appear that they came to her house either to listen to her or to talk to her; they came to talk to each other. It was sufficient satisfaction to her that they came at all. Less successful was the excellent Mrs. Chapone. She too "had her coteries, which though not sought by the young and perhaps fled from by the gay were rational, instructive and social; and it was not with self-approbation that they could ever be deserted." The appeal to the conscience which would perhaps suggest itself to no hostess in the world outside of England and New England, was re-enforced when the lady had means by the appeal to hunger. Mrs. Montagu and Mrs. Thrale supplied notoriously good food. Dr. Johnson himself understood the force of the lower motive: "I advised Mrs. Thrale, who has no card-parties at her house, to give sweet-meats and such good things in an evening as are not commonly given, and she would find company enough to come to her; for everybody loves to have things which please the palate put in their way without trouble or preparation."

If the conversation-parties of the Blue-Stockings be contrasted with those of the ladies of France they are felt at once to be relatively poor things. They are middle-class, *bornés,* provincial. The fundamental difficulty is that conversation is an art, and if the Anglo-Saxon at large has some difficulty in producing and appreciating art, the Anglo-Saxon female feels the difficulty more acutely. The end of art is unquestionably pleasure, but pleasure is a term that rouses the suspicions of the British matron. Even at the present day when the derision of the world has driven her to acknowledge "art" as one of the necessaries of civilised life, she instinctively seeks those forms of it that convey something else as well as pleasure. She prefers an oratorio to an opera, an archaic or highly mannerised picture which gives her an opportunity for study to one of direct sensuous appeal. Confronted with an undoubted work of art, her fluttered consciousness will dart hither and thither to find relief from its pure beauty in some of the outlets always afforded by a true work of art; she will not rest until she has found something to inform her mind or to fortify her character. This temperament is naturally most apt to fall into confusion when the art is so ambiguous as those that deal with the medium of words. In the matter of books she has learned, under the influence of a Gallicising generation, to speak as though she accepted literature as an art. In the matter of the drama which is largely under her patronage, the state of the stage to-day is sufficient evidence of the ease with which her attention can be distracted from the one vital question of the merit of a play as a play. And in the matter of conversation, for the brief period during which she gave it her attention, she regarded it primarily or altogether as a means of edification. To Hannah More its function was to mend the taste and form the mind; to cement friendship and to propagate Christian knowledge. Mrs. Chapone naturally took an even more sublime view of its ethical value; at its best, conversation should have as its end the spiritual communion of the participants, it should unite them in a saintly rivalry; but even dull conversation has its disciplinary value; through its agency patience and self-denial can be brought to great perfection. It is refreshing to turn from this innocent Philistinism to Dr. Johnson's purely cynical view of conversation as a game. Mrs. Chapone laid down in her *Essay on Conversation* that scandalous or uncharitable talk is a more dangerous pastime even than cards. At Mrs. Garrick's dinner-table, she exalted her theory at the expense of her practice by remarking of Mr. Thomas Hollis that "he was a bad man; he used to talk uncharitably." "Poh! poh! madam;" said the great moralist, "who is the worse for being talked of uncharitably?" The doctor himself never played at cards, and had perhaps diverted as many from them as any man in England, not by denouncing them, but by practising conversation as a fine art. When he would begin thus: "Why, Sir, as to the good or evil of card-playing—" "Now," said Garrick, "he is thinking which side he shall take." And we can fancy that many a man sat listening with delight to Dr. Johnson's defence of gaming who would otherwise have been at the tables.

The Blue-Stocking was distinguished by the propriety of her behaviour and the correctness of her sentiments. While fashionable society used the free-and-easy manners and notions of the French, middle-class ideals in England were prim. It was a reasonable age, abhorring enthusiasm. To keep cool, to retain one's self-possession, was the aim of the self-respecting lady. "Love," is a word that was not in frequent use in the eighteenth century. A lady felt at the utmost a "preference" for the man she chose to marry, and she was satisfied if she felt that he "valued" her. Mrs. Harlowe was shocked that her daughter ventured to prefer the handsome Lovelace to the repulsive Soames, —to consider (as she phrased it) "the *person*." The Blue-Stockings as a rule kept themselves admirably clear of such preferences. Mrs. Montagu at the age of twenty-two was the wife of a man of fifty-one. Mrs. Delany, the priestess of Propriety, married to oblige her family, when she was seventeen and he fifty-nine, a man whom she describes later as "altogether a person more disgusting than engaging." When she became a widow she made a second match with a man sixteen years her senior. It was hardly ladylike to marry for love. Hester Mulso did so, at the age of thirty-five, and her acquaintance took some pleasure in believing that the venture was unsuccessful. It is certain that her husband, Mr. Chapone, died after ten months of it; gossip added that he would not have his wife in the room while he lay dying. At any rate, Mrs. Chapone became an advocate of marriage by arrangement, whereas Hester Mulso had been all for the marriage of

preference. She was never weary of debating
with Richardson the case of Clarissa Harlowe
in its bearing on the two interesting questions
of filial obedience and the motive of marriage.
While she never was so heretical as to imagine
that a daughter could be at liberty to marry
against the will of her parents, she yet insisted
on that "freedom of rejection" which was all
that poor Clarissa asked. But she was far
from positing a social or mental equality of the
sexes. In her *Matrimonial Creed*, she says "I
believe that a husband has a divine right to the
absolute obedience of his wife in all cases where
the first duties do not interfere; and that as her
appointed ruler and head, he is undoubtedly
her superior." She adds naïvely that it be-
hooves a woman to select her husband carefully
in order to make sure that he is her superior
de facto as well *de jure*. But of the general
superiority of men to women she has no doubt.
"You may find advantages," she says in the
Letter to a New Married Lady, "in the conversation of many ladies, if not equal to those
that men are qualified to give, yet equal at least
to what you as a female are capable of receiving."

Mrs. Carter and Mrs. Hannah More never
married at all, their titles being brevets, after the
manner of the age. And married or unmar-

ried, these ladies kept clear of irregular relations. The philandering of Lord Lyttleton
and Lord Bath with Mrs. Montagu could
hardly with the best will in the world be made
to yield food for gossip. Dr. Johnson's ponderous gallantry and Richardson's soulful in-
timacies and Horace Walpole's sincere liking
for Hannah More were all that the Blue-Stockings had to offset the famous *liaisons* of the *salon-
iéres*. This coolness of temperament needs to
be understood before posterity can account for
the grief and horror that Mrs. Thrale's second
marriage caused among her friends.

Mrs. Thrale is to the modern mind by far
the most sympathetic of the Blue-Stockings.
She had no pose; she was witty because she
could not help it, a reader because she was fond
of books, a hostess because she liked society,
sweet-tempered because that was her nature.
She was a Welshwoman and therefore free from
the self-consciousness that blights middle-class
society in England. Her first marriage was as
purely a matter of business as the most delicate-minded could wish. Mr. Thrale admired
her but without vulgar enthusiasm. As she
herself said of him, "with regard to his wife,
though little tender of her person, he is very
partial to her understanding." Mrs. Thrale's
understanding was of a flexible, serviceable,

vital sort, ready to play and ready to work. Thrale was a prosperous brewer, but was beset by a tendency to "overbrew," which nearly ruined him. This tendency it was Mrs. Thrale's steady endeavour to check. On one occasion Thrale was drawn into a scheme to make beer "without the beggarly elements of malt and hops." In the calamity that resulted from the venture, Mrs. Thrale exerted an admirable practical faculty, borrowed money to tide over the hard times and persuaded the employees to go on with their work.

When Mr. Thrale died, his widow wound up his affairs with diligence and success and sold the brewery with a deep sigh of relief. "I have by this bargain," she wrote, "purchased peace and a stable fortune, restoration to my original rank in life, and a situation undisturbed by commercial jargon, unpolluted by commercial frauds, undisgraced by commercial connections." And then she contracted a second marriage, a marriage of inclination with Signor Piozzi, a man of character and position, whom she had known for years, a successful professional singer earning about £1200 a year. "The man I love," she said, "I love for his honesty, for his tenderness of heart, his dignity of mind, his piety to God, his duty to his mother, and his delicacy to me." It is a pity that Mrs.

Thrale could not know how entirely the nineteenth and twentieth centuries would approve her
second match; her own century was horrified
by it. Piozzi was a "foreigner," which at that
time raised a strong presumption against him.
He was an artist, and England had not yet been
laughed into hiding her conviction that to turn
from a brewer to an artist is to come down in
the world. But the really shocking thing about
Mrs. Thrale's choice of him was its frank basis
in love. She used the very word with an in-
decent freedom, assuming that it denoted a
very important element in life. Dr. Johnson's
reprobation had of course a largely personal
ground, but even Horace Walpole nicknamed
her "Mrs. Frail-Piozzi," and Madame d'Arblay brought out her worst language to express
her disillusion. "Her station in society," she
says, "her fortune, her distinguished education,
and her conscious sense of its distinction; and
yet more her high origin—a native honour,
which had always seemed the glory of her self-
appreciation; all had contributed to lift her so
eminently above the restlessly impetuous tribe
who immolate fame, interest and duty to the
shrine of passion, that the outcry of surprise
and censure raised throughout the metropolis by
these unexpected nuptials, was almost stunning
in its jarring noise of general reprobation; re-

sounding through madrigals, parodies, declamations, epigrams and irony." The marriage turned out disappointingly well. Piozzi was an agreeable, quiet, accomplished man, and took excellent care of his wife's property. Society gathered about her again, and she lived through a vivacious old age into a more congenial century. Perhaps nothing could bring home to us so sharply the changed attitude of society towards "love" than to note that this friend of Mrs. Chapone lived to talk with Tom Moore.

The Blue-Stocking lady was strongly conservative. She had all the timidities of her age, her country, her class and her sex. She had none of the indifference to public opinion of the great lady as represented by Lady Mary Wortley Montagu. She had none of the uncompromising zeal of the feminist reformer as represented by Mary Astell early in the century and by Mary Wollstonecraft at its close. She had not the free speculative mind of the brilliant lady of France. Her modest aim in life was eminently English—to gain a little personal freedom for herself and do a little good according to her lights to the persons in her immediate environment. She believed that a constitutional monarchy, the Church of England, and the superiority of man to woman enjoyed the same sanction, and that the highest. None of her activities contained a menace to any of these institutions. With an instinctive sense for what her environment would stand, she perceived that an individual here and there might study Greek or anything else, so long as she did not propose, as Mary Astell proposed, to found a college for girls on the assumption that they were as well worth teaching as boys. Her own personal adventure was enough for her. She had no wish to raise all the questions at once, as it seemed so natural to do in France, and as poor Mary Wollstonecraft insisted on doing in her deplorably un-English way. Yet she was a pioneer. She extended to women the precious right of every Englishman to do as he likes. She had the oddest resemblance to very different persons, who were to come later. It is diverting to see Miss Martineau fore-shadowed in Hannah More. What Comte was to Miss Martineau, the rector was to Mrs. More. Both women were excellent, impersonal, single-minded. The Cheap Repository Tracts that were to stem the French Revolution enjoyed the immense success that was to attend the publications of the Society for the Diffusion of Useful Knowledge. The lot of the negro stirred one as deeply as the other; to one as to the other decorum was the law of life. The difference between positivism and orthodoxy sinks into the background as we contemplate their common devotion to Propriety. Apart from so individual a case as Miss Martineau, the general class of sturdy British spinster of the nineteenth century, independent, often self-supporting, unabashed by her celibacy, turning her leisure to good account for others, rejoicing in the vicissitudes of the committee-room, constituting the spinal column of innumerable "boards," derives from Mrs. Carter and Mrs. More. The superficial view therefore that beholds the Blue-Stocking lady as merely an inferior variety of the *salonière* fails to take account of her essential character. The *salonière* was the climax of the lady as she had been understood for two thousand years; she was as far removed from ordinary womanhood as physical limitations permitted. The Blue-Stocking on the other hand began to bridge the gulf between the lady and the rest of her sex, to humanise her and to release her from mental parasitism. Her movement, blind, tentative and ineffectual as it was, became visible in the next century as a first effort in the struggle to get along without men.

THE LADY OF THE SLAVE STATES

" 'I have no prospect,' "
UNCLE ISRAEL in Mrs. Butler's *Georgian Plantation*.

TESS of the D'Urbervilles on her disastrous wedding night was carried in the arms of her somnambulist husband across the single rail that bridged a swollen stream. This singular episode may fairly be taken as a symbol of proprietary marriage; there are moments when every married woman finds that she is borne in the arms of a sleep-walker. She dares not wake him as he foots his dangerous way, for it might mean destruction to both. If the lady's life everywhere is punctuated by crises in which she must shut her eyes and take her chance, an even more violent figure must be used to typify her existence at a special time and place when her suspense and danger were not momentary but chronic. According to the social theory of the old South, the lady's equilibrium was that of a Gothic saint in her niche; she stood at a giddy height but the fabric beneath her was solidly buttressed; nothing short of an earthquake could displace her.

In reality, however, she was neither more nor less secure than the lady-acrobat. Flat on his back on the ground lay Quashy with lifted legs, and on his upturned soles stood with folded arms the planter. And on the planter's head stood the lady, gracefully poised on one toe. The spectator's heart is in his mouth as he sees her with infinite precautions bend her body forward, stretch out the balancing leg behind and extend her arms. She seems to be flying like the Victory of Paeonius at Olympia. She is an angel. But though she is smiling her eye is fixed and her attention strained. Quashy has but to turn over, well she knows, and her brave defiance of gravitation will come to grief.

The archaic character of southern antebellum society is illustrated by the rapidity with which since its collapse it has fled back in historical perspective to join the forms with which it should properly have been contemporary. It disappeared not as things so widespread generally disappear in real life, a little at a time and so gradually that the participants hardly notice the change. On the contrary it disappeared as things do in dreams; it was held together like M. Valdemar by mesmeric passes and when they were interrupted it was found to have been dead some time. It became immediately the theme of legend as though it had

thriven in the ninth century instead of in the
nineteenth. Like most other archaic social
forms it has left but an unsatisfying document-
ary basis for history. For the hundredth time
fiction is proved to be incomparably more enduring than life, and *Uncle Tom's Cabin* bids
fair to be the form in which posterity will see
the age of which it is so bewildering a mixture
of *Dichtung und Wahrheit*. The Homeric
poems and the romances of chivalry, the Hebrew
scriptures and *Uncle Tom* have established
ideas against which the scientific historian, if
we may assume his existence, can but file his
exceptions; the jury will not heed his techni-
calities. The South cried out against *Uncle
Tom* but was unable to oppose it by a similarly
persuasive work of fiction, and fiction appears
to be the only form of statement that in the long
run carries conviction. As far as the voice of
the South itself has been effective in helping to
shape the myth, it has spoken chiefly through
the lips of amiable and estimable old ladies re-
calling honestly but uncritically the days of
their youth. This is a class of literature in
which notoriously dimensions expand and
colours grow bright. After a course of it the
reader who visits the physical remains of its
world is amazed by their shrinkage. At Monti-
cello and Mount Vernon the traveller feels, it

is true, a touching and imperishable charm, but it is the charm of modesty, not the charm of grandeur. And apart from the historic seats of the mighty he searches in vain for the stately mansions of his fancy. Surely they were not all burned by Yankee raiders or riotous freedmen. "Stately mansions" is in fact very strong language. The traveller would not immediately recognise as deserving it the large two-storied house of wood or brick with its double gallery that formed the well-to-do-planter's residence.

The archaic lady of the South obeyed a law of her being in leaving very little written record of herself. Ladies from the real world penetrated into her territory from time to time and gave accounts of what they saw. Two Englishwomen could hardly be more unlike in temperament and antecedents than Miss Martineau and Fanny Kemble, but they differed far more from the Southern lady than from each other. They agreed in approaching the South with a lively interest and each was stirred to write excellently in her own way of what she found. In the North a rather remarkable group of women arose in the second quarter of the nineteenth century, able to think and to speak, who associated, with a profounder logic than they were perhaps themselves aware of, the political and social limitations of women with those of the slave. A really noble eloquence sprang from the enthusiasm of Lucretia Mott. The lady of the South was equally enthusiastic. The time came when she sincerely believed that the chief end of slavery was the good of the slave. But she was unable to say so. She could suffer for her faith, see her sons die for it, cherish it long after the men who fought for it had laid it aside, but it never stirred her to effective defence of it. This is not attributable to any inherent defect in it; causes just as bad have been movingly and triumphantly argued. It is not attributable to any lack on the part of the Southern lady of the talents that we call literary, for soon after the war she gained a creditable place among American men and women of letters. The trouble was that the social system based on slavery discouraged general mental effort both in men and women, but especially in women. Professor Shaler has worked out very convincingly the effect on Southern manners, culture and history of the survival in the South of feudal habits of minds, and Professor Trent has added, in his life of Simms, the direct result of these habits in the discouragement of self-expression. "Southerners lived a life which, though simple and picturesque, was nevertheless calculated to repress many of the best faculties and powers of our nature. It was a life affording few opportunities to talents that did not lie in certain beaten grooves. It was a life gaining its intellectual nourishment, just as it did its material comforts, largely from abroad,—a life that choked all thought and investigation that did not tend to conserve existing institutions and opinions, a life that rendered originality scarcely possible except under the guise of eccentricity." In other words the planter's high gifts of intelligence were concentrated on keeping his balance, and the lady in an even higher degree must make no gesture outside her prescribed rôle. Though the exigencies of the situation often made him a shrewd debater and a vigorous orator, they had no analogous effect upon his wife.

The truth is that in the days of slavery nobody was free at the South. The planter whose autocracy was his boast, who contrasted himself with the men of other communities as being more completely a free agent than they, submitted to enact laws for himself that no other Anglo-Saxon society in the world at that time would have endured. It may not be surprising that Louisiana with its exotic social ideas should make "imprisonment at hard labour not less than three years nor more than twenty-one years, or death, at the discretion of the court," the punishment for one who "shall make use of language in any public discourse . . . or in private discourses . . . or shall make use of signs or actions having a tendency to produce discontent among the free coloured population of this state, or to excite insubordination among the slaves." But it is hard to believe that the Code of Virginia of 1849 abridged the freedom of speech and press. As the slave was a chattel of the owner who could do what he liked with him except kill him (otherwise than "by accident in giving such slave moderate correction") it would seem evident that he could if he liked set him free. In Virginia he could generally do so, by his last will or by deed, provided his creditors were not prejudiced; though the Revised Code attached to the permission to emancipate a rider that contained the oddest *rapprochement* of barbarism and civilisation: "If any emancipated slave (infants excepted) shall remain within the state more than twelve months after his or her right to freedom shall have accrued, he or she shall forfeit all such right, and may be apprehended and sold by the overseers of the poor, etc., for the benefit of the Literary Fund." But in several states an act of legislature was required to allow a man to relinquish his property. In Georgia the penalty for attempting to free a slave in any other way was not to exceed one thousand dollars.

In the use of his chattel the owner was hampered in many ways by laws forbidding him to teach the slave to read or write. In Georgia anyone was liable to fine and imprisonment "who shall procure, suffer or permit a slave, negro or person of colour to transact business for him in writing."

All these abridgments of liberty which would at that period have been intolerable to most English-speaking people were but the reflection of a far more coercive social sentiment. The lawlessness of the planter in certain directions may be recognised as reaction against the restrictions on which his existence as a class depended. No man was ever more enslaved by public opinion. As the last traces of serfdom and slavery vanished in other societies, the planters came gradually to realise that they were alone in the world. They were mutineers against the course of civilisation, and the only safety of mutineers is to hang together lest they hang separately. Thus a rigorous and imperative social mandate was formulated more tyrannous than the statute-book, and another mediæval characteristic was revivified. Nothing so "solid" had existed since the effective days of the Holy Roman Empire. Once more the world saw a society so homogeneous that if one turned over all must. Every planter must continue steadfastly to hold his wolf by the ears, or all must let go together. The homogeneity of the middle age in thought, in art and in *Weltanschauung* was in the last analysis the result of fear, the fear of eternal damnation systematised and exploited by the church and the fear of violence from every secular power strong enough to offer it. Perhaps no social motive but fear has ever had so strong a cohesive power. The solidity of the South before the war was a striking example of its strength. The South was afraid of a number of things;—of Nat Turner and his kind, of the repressive force of Northern opinion, but most of all of the disintegrating effect on its own members of free discussion, of a liberal habit of mind, of participation in the current of thought of the world at large. The planter was forced to build his moral house for defence, as the baron of the twelfth century was forced to build his physical house. Light and air were necessarily sacrificed to the requirements of fortification. The history of the middle age is largely a history of the growth of walls induced by the improvements in the machinery of assault. So is the history of the slaveholding South. As the castellan developed his means of defence from the simple wall and tower to the mathematical complexity of the twelfth century fortress, so the planter developed his moral position as the attack became more systematic; and every addition to his defences meant increased isolation. The South was always addicted to religion: when the sects that chiefly ministered to it broke from their brethren in the North and preached slavery as the will of God, we may say that the portcullis fell. When under the planter's orders the Southern postmaster refused to transmit through the United States mails so mild an anti-slavery influence as the *New York Tribune,* we see the raising of the pont-levis. Fear begets courage in well-bred men and women, but it is a courage of a somewhat self-conscious order and has inevitably the narrow aim of self-preservation. Neither the baron nor the planter had much time to give to mental and spiritual culture. The brightest powers of the one were devoted to the art of war, of the other to the art of debate. If slavery was to persist its champions must uphold it incessantly in the Senate and on the election-platform. The whole brains of the South were applied for fifty years to the mediæval task of erecting a logic and an ethic for slavery. This was as stimulating and exciting to the planter as was the theory and practice of resisting siege to the castellan, but what sort of life did it offer to the lady?

It is generally remarked that a woman,

whether by some real psychological idiosyncrasy or as a result of her ordinary conditions of life, is apt to be more struck with details than by generalisations. This sometimes works to her own disadvantage and that of the community, as for instance when it makes her the supporter of the "bargain-counter." Her abstract knowledge of the principles of this phenomenon is not sufficiently vivid to enable her to withstand the appeal of a concrete instance. On the other hand this feminine trait is of inestimable service as society is now constituted in keeping its owner incorrigibly individualistic, easily interested in the special case, ready to ignore the law when it is inept and thus to constitute herself a perpetual court of equity. Bearing in mind this function characteristic of all women and more especially of the lady, the student of slavery is baffled by the difficulty of understanding how the planter's theories were able to convince his wife in the presence of their practical results. Fanny Kemble writes: "Mr.—— was called out this evening to listen to a complaint of overwork from a gang of pregnant women. I did not stay to listen to the details of their petition, for I am unable to command myself on such occasions, and Mr.—— seemed positively degraded in my eyes as he stood enforcing upon these women the necessity of fulfilling their appointed tasks. How honourable he would have appeared to me begrimed with the sweat and toil of the coarsest manual labour, to what he then seemed, setting forth to these wretched, ignorant women, as a duty, their unpaid, exacting labour! I turned away in bitter disgust." How did it happen that any gentlewoman was able to command herself on such occasions? We are accustomed to think that our own social sins endure chiefly because the lady sees so little of them. In every case others do the dirty work for her. If she had to shoot and skin her own bird the plumage would disappear from her hat. A military journal has lately cried out against the proposition to send out a woman as war-correspondent. If the world begins to learn through women what goes on at the front (cries this voice in the wilderness) we may as well say good-bye to war! Similarly if the sweatshop, the tenement house and the "Raines-law hotel" were picturesquely grouped under the elms of her country-place, if her children spent their infancy in close playfellowship with the offspring of those institutions, if her husband were occasionally called out from his dinner to listen to a complaint of overwork from a gang of pregnant women, we like to imagine that the result would be a clean sweep of this class of our iniquities.

One answer to the puzzle in regard to the planter's wife is fairly obvious. The most vocal part of the South was Virginia. Nine persons out of ten in the North to-day use "Virginia" and "the South" as interchangeable terms. That state formed early the habit of producing distinguished men; the prestige of her revolutionary history gave her great weight both North and South. The South (with the exception perhaps of South Carolina) was willing to make Virginia the spokesman and the North was willing to accept her as representative. But Virginia was not representative. When an old Virginian recalls with rapture those rosy ante-bellum days which have become something of a jest to a world that knew them not, he is not touching up the picture very much as regards the relation between master and servant. It is probably true that at any rate after the soil was eaten up the worst features of slavery were not visible in Virginia. A lady might live and die there without once seeing a negro under the lash, or even witnessing unless in exceptional circumstances those forcible partings of families which the abolitionist rightly put his finger on as the greatest of social mistakes. She was surrounded by a community of sleek, wellfed, cheerful, comic creatures, as unlike Fanny Kemble's retinue as two groups

of the same race could be. In her neighbourhood harsh treatment of servants was bad form
and was punished by social ostracism. And
if the Virginian emigrated to another state he
took his traditions with him. If his neighbours in the new environment had a lower
standard they concealed it from him as long as
possible. "I cannot," said Thomas Dabney,
expressing a profound truth in social psychology, "I cannot punish people with whom I associate every day." The average Virginia
gentleman could no more have a slave flogged
than the average gentleman anywhere could de-
liberately infect a fellow-creature with tuber-
culosis. We are so made that our victims must
be out of our sight. But he could and did
breed and rear strong, healthy men and women
whom it would do you good to see, and sell
them in large annual invoices for service in the
sugar and cotton states. A Virginia gentleman
told Olmsted that "his women were uncom-
monly good breeders; he did not suppose there
was a lot of women anywhere that bred faster
than his," and Rhodes notes a lady in Baltimore,
"richly and fashionably dressed, and apparently
moving in the best society, who derived her income from the sale of children of a half-dozen
negro women she owned, although their husbands belonged to other masters." But in the

consciousness of the owner of a human stock-
farm, and still more of the owner's wife, there
was a sincere contempt for the next link in the
chain, the slave-trader and the auctioneer; while
the overseer, the actual slave-driver of the cot-
ton-field, the man who did the dirty work on
which the whole social scheme depended, was
despised by all.   In fact the lady of the plantation felt toward the overseer by whose exertions she lived, as the lady of other economic
dispensations feels toward the proprietor of the
sweat-shop whose product is on her back.

All the conditions that bore hardly on the man
of talent were equally operative on the woman,
and she had a special extinguisher of her own
in the nature of the planter's conception of the
lady.   Her man did not wish her to be clever.
There is at the first glance no obvious reason
why the Southern lady should not have been a
salonière; the type is sufficiently aristocratic
and exclusive, one would think, to recommend
it to the gregarious and leisured planter.   The
student is surprised to find that on the contrary
the married woman had virtually no social existence.   The woman of Southern romance is
the young girl; the social intercourse of the little Southern cities consisted chiefly of balls and
dances at which the young girl might be seen
by young men.   When she was married, her

husband carried her to his plantation, and there
she lived in isolation. She reverted to a far
earlier type than that of *salonière,* the type
namely of the twelfth century chatelaine. Only
the few who maintained town-houses as well as
country-houses and spent part of every year in
Richmond or Charleston or New Orleans retained their hold upon communion with their
kind, and for them a staid and modified social
life was deemed fitting. For them the dance
was over. Instead of being the means of a
wider freedom, marriage was an abdication.
Mrs. Gilman in her *Recollections of a Southern Matron* describes the ideal lady of the
plantation. "Mamma possessed more than
whole acres of charms, for though not brilliant
she was good-tempered and sensible. A demure
look and reserved manner concealed a close
habit of observation. She would sit in company for hours, making scarcely a remark, and
recollect afterwards every fact that had been
stated, to the colour of a riband or the stripe
of a waistcoat. Home was her true sphere;
there everything was managed with prompti-
tude and decision and papa, who was . . .
an active planter was glad to find his domestic
arrangements quiet and orderly. No one ever
managed an establishment better; but there was
no appeal from her opinions, and I have known

her even eloquent in defending a recipe. . . . Her sausages were pronounced to be the best flavoured in the neighbourhood; her hog's cheese was delicacy itself; her preserved watermelons were carved with the taste of a sculptor."

When the heroine of the work was herself married she remarked that the planter's bride "dreams of an independent sway over her household, devoted love and unbroken intercourse with her husband, and indeed longs to be released from the eyes of others, that she may dwell only beneath the sunbeam of his."

If we turn to so romantic an account of Southern ante-bellum society as is contained in (for instance) Kennedy's *Swallow Barn,* we find a marked sentimental discrimination between the young girl and the matron. Lovely maidens are portrayed, brown and blond, madcap and demure. Their manners, their whims, their dresses are important. Their love-affairs are the excitement of the countryside. But the matron, the respected head of the establishment, is touched in with something of satire. Her good qualities and achievements are duly set down; her affairs are said to go like clockwork; she rises with the lark and infuses vigour into her recalcitrant assistants. But her charms are not the author's theme. "She is a thin woman to look upon and a feeble; with a sallow complexion, and a pair of animated black eyes which impart a portion of fire to a countenance otherwise demure from the paths worn across it in the frequent travel of a low-country ague." Her contribution to social enjoyment seems to have consisted in playing the harpsichord for the children to dance and in singing *The Rose-tree in Full Bearing.* For the rest, her annalist to describe her foibles dips his pen in some medium which from the old-fashioned acidity of its flavour might be the lady's own blackberry cordial. She takes more pride (says he) in her leechcraft than becomes a Christian woman, and prepares daily doses for the helpless youngsters of the family, both white and black. And there is an element of the mystical in some of her prescriptions: "Nine scoops of water in the hollow of the hand, from the sycamore spring, for three mornings, before sunrise, and a cup of strong coffee with lemon-juice, will break an ague, try it when you will." Her husband laughs at her and depends upon her.

It is fair to say that *Swallow Barn* was written before the *femme de trente ans* had become domesticated in English literature. Mr. Page, writing in an age in which she is fully appreciated, feels it incumbent upon him to celebrate with more enthusiasm the lady of the plantation. Very charmingly he does it, yet in his page as plain as in Kennedy's stands the record of her limitations. Her life was on its professional side the life of the Greek lady. The programme laid down by Ischomachus for his child-bride governed the days of the later mistress of slaves. Each was the wife and steward of a farmer. Each was responsible for the reception in the house of produce of the farm intended for home consumption. Each must keep order regnant among slaves and goods. A surprising amount of what the household used was in each case made under the lady's direction from raw material produced on the estate. The Greek lady worked with wool, the modern lady with cotton, but each must understand spinning and weaving, shaping and sewing. Each was the chief executive of a large and motley community, in duty bound to enforce the laws. And each was responsible for the health of her household; it was her duty to prevent sickness if possible, and when it came to tend it. Each doubtless if not overtaxed derived satisfaction from the performance of important work bearing directly on the welfare and happiness of those she loved best, but neither could be called a free woman. In the case of the Greek lady we see this plainly enough. No sentiment had arisen in her day to mask the issue. If she was constrained to an exacting profession no one obscured the fact by calling her a queen, or with a much stronger connotation of leisure, an angel. In the case of the lady of the plantation we are misled by her husband's vocabulary, which is that of the twelfth century. It is hard to realise that he could combine the manner and phrases of the minnesinger with the practice of the ancient Athenian. In some aspects the law-abiding and thrifty Athenian was the better husband of the two; for the planter indemnified himself for the fear he felt for his order by a careless courage in regard to his individual life, and for the lack in his existence of some of the ordinary sources of interest by the speculative habit. Thus he might shoot or be shot somewhat casually, and he might lose at cards anything from his wife's most valued house-servant to the cotton-crop for the year after next.

One of the great burdens of slavery was that it overworked the lady. She was typically undervitalised. Mr. Page in the full swing of his dithyrambic declares that she was "often delicate and feeble in frame, and of a nervous organisation so sensitive as to be a great sufferer." Mrs. Smedes, who has left us so beautiful a picture of the best type of plantation life, complains of the heavy drain it made upon the vitality of the ruling class. "There were others who felt that slavery was a yoke upon the white man's neck almost as galling as on the slave's; and it was a saying that the mistress of a plantation was the most complete slave on it. I can testify to the truth of this in my mother's life and experience. There was no hour of the day that she was not called upon to minister to their real or imaginary wants. Who can wonder that we longed for a lifting of the incubus, and that in the family of Thomas Dabney the first feeling, when the war was ended, was of joy that one dreadful responsibility, at least, was removed?" It is quite plain from the record that Mrs. Dabney, mistress of hundreds of slaves, the happy wife of a faithful husband, died of nervous exhaustion. She was overworked. A slaveholder could not get rid of an unprofitable servant. The good abolitionist in Boston believed that if the omelette was scorched, Mammy Venus was strung up by the thumbs to receive forty lashes; but the owner of slaves was after all a man with bowels like another. He could not flog a person with whom he associated every day. It was the slave who traded on the softness of a good master, as we may learn from an instructive little episode in the Dabney family.

"After the mistress had passed away, Alcey resolved that she would not cook any more, and she took her own way of getting assigned to field work. She systematically disobeyed orders, and stole or destroyed the greater part of the provisions given her for the table. No special notice was taken, so she resolved to show more plainly that she was tired of the kitchen. Instead of getting the chickens for dinner from the coop as usual she unearthed from some corner an old hen that had been sitting for six weeks, and served her up as a fricassée! We had company to dinner that day; that would have deterred most of the servants but not Alcey. She achieved her object, for she was sent to the field the next day, without so much as a reprimand, if I remember rightly."

At a time when timidity in the North and fear in the South ruled conversation, good Miss Martineau trod heavily through American society, asking terrible questions and making observations hardly less startling than obvious. Some deliberate fictions were poured into her ear-trumpet, which she was unable to check as another might have done to whom general conversation was audible; and sometimes doubtless she misunderstood what was said to her. But if her ears were not always trustworthy, her eyes enjoyed a compensating power. She passed two years in this country, devoting five months to a tour of the Southern states,—Maryland, Virginia, the Carolinas, Georgia, Alabama, Louisiana, Kentucky and Tennessee. She was everywhere kindly received and found the planter ready and willing to talk of the chief circumstance of his life. Fanny Kemble, five years later, decided to set down nothing in her plantation journal that was not the result of her own observation, because she had heard people boasting how gloriously they had gulled Miss Martineau. But it will hardly be supposed that any slave-owner exerted his powers of mystification to give the stranger an unduly dark view of the peculiar institution; if we are to read her narrative with allowance for misinformation wilfully supplied, our confidence must be least in the passages most favourable to slavery.

Miss Martineau was astonished, as other travellers were, by the hardships of the lady of the plantation. She must rise early and but late take rest. A comfortable house is to be had only as the result of systematic arrangement, but systematic arrangement was impossible to slaves. The Englishwoman stood aghast at seeing so many servants accomplish so little. She would have preferred to serve herself rather than wait for the tardy and ineffective service of the blacks. She found them lolling against the bed-posts before she was up in the morning, leaning against sofas through the house during the day, officiously offering service at every turn and generally making a mess of it. She found little real comfort in the planter's house, and said indeed in her downright way that with one exception she never saw a clean room or bed within the boundaries of the slave-states. She saw the lady without leisure save as it was bought at the price of despair and a momentary determination to let things go. She saw the great bunch of keys at the lady's girdle in constant requisition, for everything consumable must be locked up, and yet must be forthcoming at the whimsical demand of minis-trants whose orbits were incalculable. She saw the lady constrained to follow up personally every order she gave lest the result be confusion. She found and noted many remarkable women whose powers were equal to their responsibil-ities, women competent to rule over a little barbarous society, who realised the gravity of the duty that lay upon them to watch over the health and regulate the lives of a number of persons who could in no wise take care of them-selves. Often she found a lady who was un-equal to her task, timid, languid and unintelli-gent. The house of that woman would not be a pleasant one in which to stay. But in the main she was impressed by the lady's capacity for making the best of a system for which she was not responsible and of which she was the garlanded victim.

Miss Martineau had no hesitation in asking any lady she met for a candid expression of opinion of the system, and some very singular confessions were poured into the sympathetic ear-trumpet, if it reported truly to its ingenuous owner. Two ladies, "the distinguishing ornaments of a very superior society," were very unhappy and told their new friend what a curse they found slavery to be. A planter's wife, in the bitterness of her heart, declared that she was but "the chief slave of the harem." One singular little anecdote shows how the lady's logic could work to her husband's credit. "One sultry morning I was sitting with a friend who was giving me all manner of information about her husband's slaves. While we were talking one of the house slaves passed us. I observed that she appeared superior to all the rest; to which my friend assented. 'She is A's wife?' said I. 'We call her A's wife but she has never been married to him. A and she came to my husband five years ago and asked him to let them marry: but he could not allow it, because he had not made up his mind whether to sell A; and he hates parting husband and wife.

They have four children but my husband has never been able to let them marry; he has not determined yet whether he shall sell A.' "

Another story is irresistible in this connection, though it came to Miss Martineau at one remove. A Southern lady told a group of friends the romantic story of a pretty mulatto girl whom she had once owned. A young man came to stay at her house who fell in love with the girl. The girl fled to her mistress for protection and received it. Some weeks later the young man came again, saying that he was so desperately in love with the girl he could not live without her. "I pitied the young man," concluded the lady, "so I sold the girl to him for $1500."

The characteristic virtue of the lady of the plantation, Miss Martineau found to be patience. Only the native, born and bred among slaves, achieved it in perfection. Foreigners or Northerners who became slaveholders could not compass it; they were impatient and sometimes severe; their tempers broke down altogether; their nerves were racked and their self-control shattered by the unconquerable inertia of the slave. But the mistress born in slavery hardly noticed that the company were waiting twenty minutes for the second course, and was willing to repeat an order unto seventy times seven. A certain amount of lying and stealing, of disobedience and procrastination, was allowed the slave daily with his other rations.

No problem-novel could be more interesting than the true narrative of the experiences of Frances Anne Kemble in connection with slavery. This young woman was of a strongly individualistic type, being not only English but a Kemble and an artist. Her appearance on the stage, followed by immediate popularity, had saved her father's theatre from insolvency. London petted her; people of importance recognised her importance. After a triumphant tour of the United States she made a love-match with Mr. Pierce Butler of Philadelphia, and in the winter of 1838-9 she with her two little children accompanied her husband to his plantations in Georgia. She had contemplated the theory of slavery with entire distaste as she admitted in a letter written before she began her journey: "Assuredly I am going prejudiced against slavery, for I am an Englishwoman" (it was precisely five years since slavery had been abolished in Jamaica, and the slave-trade that had filled the Southern colonies with negroes had been continued by the British government in the face of earnest prayers from the colonies that it might be stopped) "in whom the absence of such a prejudice would be disgraceful. Nevertheless, I go prepared to find many mitigations in the practice to the general injustice and cruelty of the system—much kindness on the part of the masters, much content on the part of the slaves." This impetuous and able young woman, not only warmhearted but highly intelligent, was forced by her qualities to judge for herself of the system by which she and her children were supported. Incidentally she was forced to judge her husband, and as all the world knows, she finally went back to her own people. Her *Journal of a Residence on a Georgian Plantation* naturally deals only gingerly with her personal relations. It is easy enough to fill in the details of the bewilderment of both young people, the irritation and dismay of the planter as his uncontrollable wife went about the estates cheerfully teaching insubordination to the hands, and the panic of the wife when she discovered that her husband was sincerely unconvinced of sin toward his black people. The two estates, one devoted to cotton, the other to rice, had long been in the hands of overseers, unvisited by a master. The pecuniary returns had been satisfactory, and the plantations had a good repute as being well-managed. But they were very different from the long-established homestead plantations of Virginia. On the rice-plantation the planter's residence consisted of "three small rooms and three still smaller, which would be more appropriately designated as closets, a wooden recess by way of pantry, and a kitchen detached from the dwelling—a mere wooden out-house, with no floor but the bare earth, and for furniture a congregation of filthy negroes, who lounge in and out of it like hungry hounds at all hours of the day and night, picking up such scraps of food as they can find about, which they discuss squatting down upon their hams. Of our three apartments, one is our sitting, eating and living room, and is sixteen feet by fifteen. The walls are plastered indeed, but neither papered nor painted; it is divided from our bedroom by a dingy wooden partition covered all over with hooks, pegs and nails, to which hats, caps, keys, etc., are suspended in graceful irregularity. The doors open by means of wooden latches, raised by means of small bits of packthread—I imagine the same primitive order of fastening celebrated in the touching chronicle of Red Riding Hood; how they shut I will not attempt to describe, as the shutting of a door is a process of extremely rare occurrence throughout the whole Southern country. The third room, a chamber with sloping ceiling, immediately over our sitting room and under the roof, is appropriated to the nurse and my two babies.

Of the closets, one is the overseer's bedroom, the other his office, and the third, adjoining our bedroom, is Mr.——'s dressing room and *cabinet d'affaires,* where he gives audiences to the negroes, redresses grievances, distributes red woollen caps, shaves himself, and performs the other offices of his toilet. Such being our abode, I think you will allow there is little danger of my being dazzled by the luxurious splendours of a Southern slave residence."

The plantation was in fact not a home but an industrial plant. In visiting it the planter expected such hardships as the owner of a western mine might have to encounter to-day. This is not the type of plantation that lends itself to romantic treatment; it is not what the Southern lady thinks of when she describes the elegance of the life of her youth. But it was a well accredited and very common type in the rice and cotton states, and must be taken into account as fully as the other. Many a lady lived on such a plantation without mental suffering, or at any rate without expressing such suffering, and we can only guess in the absence of her testimony at the reasons for her ease of mind.

Mrs. Butler paid visits to the ladies of neighbouring plantations and found that they lived in no greater luxury than she. The grounds were shaggy and unkempt, the houses "ruinous, rack-rent and tumble-down." Traversing one day a charming woodride which divided two estates, her mind "not unnaturally dwelt upon the terms of deadly feud in which the two families own-ing them are living with each other. A hor-rible quarrel has occurred quite lately upon the subject of the ownership of this very ground I was skirting, between Dr. H. and young Mr. W.; they have challenged each other. The terms have appeared as a sort of advertisement in the local paper, and are to the effect that they are to fight at a certain distance with certain weapons— firearms, of course; that there is to be on the per-son of each a white paper, or mark, immediately over the region of the heart, as a point for di-rect aim; and whoever kills the other is to have the privilege of cutting off his head and stick-ing it up on a pole on the piece of land which was the origin of the debate." In the sequel it appears there was no duel, but Dr. H., meet-ing his enemy by chance in an hotel shot him dead upon the spot.

In paying her visits, Mrs. Butler, like Miss Martineau, plunged by preference into the most delicate of questions. How can you stand slavery? she would genially ask her hostess. Where the answers are recorded, the ladies seem naturally enough to have shirked the question of abstract justice and to have argued, on the assumption of the inevitability of slavery, that kindness and indulgence were so common among masters as to make the slave's life far happier in practice than in theory. Mrs. Butler makes a shrewd comment which goes far to solve the whole problem. "They" (women) "are very seldom just, and are generally treated with more indulgence than justice by men." In Mrs. Butler's own reflections, her personal helplessness is the obstacle she comes up against when she tries to help the helpless slave. An intelligent boy of sixteen asked her to teach him to read. To do so was to break the law under which she lived, and though she would probably not have boggled at mere law-breaking, she was embarrassed by the consideration that her husband would have to pay the fines which she would incur for the first and second offenses. The third offense was punishable by imprisonment. She sighed to think that she could not begin with Aleck's third lesson so that the penalty might light on the right shoulders. She winds up by saying, "I certainly intend to teach Aleck to read. I certainly won't tell Mr.—— anything about it. I'll leave him to find it out, as slaves, and servants, and children, and all oppressed and ignorant and uneducated and unprincipled people

do; then, if he forbids me, I can stop—perhaps
before then the lad may have learned his letters."
This brilliant and energetic young woman who
had demonstrated her ability to maintain herself
in economic independence, found herself suddenly reduced to the stereotyped movements of
the lady-acrobat; a spontaneous gesture would
topple her husband over.

The general statement that the lady of the
South in the early thirties had but little to say
for herself might seem to a reader of Mrs. Gilman's *Southern Matron* to need modification.
This amiable and somewhat amusing work
hangs, upon a thread of love-story, a series of
miniatures. The revolutionary grandfather,
the father who was a Harvard graduate, the
mother whom we must make the most of as one
of the few recorded ladies of the time, the young
girl who tells the tale and whose adventures
glow with an importance conceded not only by
this book but by the society which existed for
the purpose of getting her married, the somewhat disillusioned but philosophical matron,
all are endowed by Mrs. Gilman with the high
colour, the almost superhuman elegance which
the miniature-painter's sitter has always expected as his money's worth. There can be no
doubt that Mrs. Gilman's subjects would be delighted to have posterity believe they looked

just as she presents them. Their charming pro-
files are not projected against a stormy sky; no
hint is given that their world is not as durable
as delicate. Here, then, the pleased reader is
inclined to say, is a portrait of the Southern
lady's life painted by herself; how delightful
a life it was and how skilfully she renders it!
The system of education described in the work
itself seems somewhat unsatisfactory, but what
more could one ask of a system than that it
should produce girls so competent as this one
to express themselves? It is a disappointment
when further research shows that Mrs. Gilman
was born in Boston and came to Charleston as
the wife of a Unitarian minister. It is New
England, charmed and subjugated, that voices
the sentiment of the Carolinas. Her description of the education of girls remains where it
was, but its fairest fruit proves to have been fastened upon it like an apple on a Christmas-tree.

"Mamma" (says the heroine of the book) had
been an "Edisto belle," but when the curtain
rises she had entered upon her second stage.
The children's education had been carried on
chiefly at home,—altogether in the case of the
girls. As they grew older they hazed their
governess out of the house, with the high spirit
becoming their masterful race. Papa shook his
riding-whip playfully at the culprits and ad-

vertised for a man. An ignorant and incompetent youth from Connecticut applied and for some unexplained reason was accepted. When his brief term came to a violent end, papa resolved to educate his children himself. For the first three days they were very amiable, he very paternal; on the fourth John was turned out of the room, Richard was pronounced a mule, and Cornelia went sobbing to mamma, while papa said he might be compelled to ditch rice-fields but he would never undertake to teach children again.

Then mamma tried her hand. Her own education had not been wide and she wisely limited her subjects of instruction to reading, writing and spelling. Mamma already combined the activities of the matron of an orphan asylum where the orphans' ages ranged from one minute to a hundred years, of a physician in good practice and of the keeper of a country-store. Hardly had she said "Spell irrigate," when the coachman appeared to ask for the key to the oat-bin. Chloe came next for a dose of calomel for Syphax. Then Maum Phillis brought in "little maussa" to nurse. Lafayette and Venus fell out over their work and mamma must arbitrate. A field hand who had received a cut in his ankle from a hoe was brought into the hall, and mamma must minister to him. She inspected the great foot, covered with blood and sweat, superintended a bath, prepared an application, extracted some dirt from the wound and bandaged it. Mammy Phillis sent some eggs for sale and Daddy Ajax reported that he had broken the axe and requisitioned a new one. While this last matter was under discussion, the dinner-horn sounded. That evening a party of visitors arrived for a week's stay, and thus ended mamma's effort as governess. In the interest of romance the next instructor was a beautiful though consumptive youth from New England with the forehead of the period, "rising in its white mass like a tower of mind." This young man covered the field of human knowledge, except the French language, which was imparted by one to whom it was native, but whose "conscience only embraced externals." Papa was satisfied if he paid round sums for education, and mamma was easy if the teachers seemed busy. The tutor rambled in the woods with his fair charge, fell in love with her, and, most honourably allowing concealment to feed upon his lungs, returned home to die.

When the little girl who was afterwards to be Mrs. Roger A. Pryor was not yet ten years old the aunt with whom she lived realised the shortcomings of education on the plantation

and took up her residence in Charlottesville,
which was then beginning to be the centre of a
little group of cultivated people. The child
was entered at the Female Seminary. The
headmaster examined her and prescribed her
lessons. The books given her were Aber-
crombie's *Intellectual Philosophy,* Watts' *Improvement of the Mind,* Goldsmith's *History of
Greece* and somebody's *Natural Philosophy.*
A more advanced little student blazed the trail
for the child through these works, enclosing in
brackets the briefest possible answers to the
questions in Watts. Thus the little girl was enabled with labour and tears to say (when asked
"What is logic?"), "Logic is the art of investi-
gating and communicating Truth." After a
few months in the seminary she was removed
by the good aunt, and home education began
again. She read classical English literature
with her aunt, she learned French from a German, and she studied music under the direction
of an itinerant master whose relations with the
sheriff made it often convenient for him to appear at midnight to give a lesson.

Young Charles Dabney, writing to his father
from the University of Virginia, expresses his
pleasure that a governess has been secured for
his sister Sarah. "Let her," says the pompous
and high-minded collegian, " have every oppor-

tunity; and do not think that because she is a woman any kind of education will be sufficient for her to keep house. I know you do not think this, yet there are many who constantly say that a woman ought not to be well educated,—that any kind of education will be enough for a house-keeper, and that a very intelligent and accomplished woman is likely to make a bad wife."

A special piquancy is lent to the spectacle of the lady as mistress of slaves by a knowledge of her history, a review of which might be fitly entitled "Up from Slavery." Herr Bebel in his striking way declares that woman was the first slave, "she was a slave before the slave existed." The gradual promotion of an occasional slave to comparative idleness began to make a lady of her. When she was given control over other slaves and when she was considered to be her master's wife in some special sense which differentiated her from the other women who bore him children, the process was complete. Her idleness consisted in release from useful manual labour, and was an evidence of her husband's wealth. As such it was valuable to him, and she preserved it at his command. Not only was she excused from labour, —she was forbidden it. The Chinese, a logical and direct people, cripple the little girls of the gentle class so that they may bear the outward visible sign of incapacity to labour. The hampering dress of the European lady has the same purpose. The etiquette which everywhere forbids the lady to serve herself is closely bound up with her husband's *amour propre*. He believes that his objection to seeing his wife occupied in useful toil is sheer consideration of the strong for the weak, whereas it is largely based on the fear that her exertions will reflect on his ability to compete with other men for the prizes of life. The lady of the proprietary household is therefore as much under orders as any of her subordinates, but her orders are not to work with her hands. This by no means dispenses her from other labour. She uses more nervous energy in causing a task to be done by incompetent servants than it would cost her to do it herself, but she is not allowed to do it herself. In the presence of slavery,—in Constantinople, for instance, or in South Carolina, —the performance of manual labour would be of course more shameful than elsewhere. Writers dealing with the old South, naturally struck with its feudalistic survivals, are inclined to dwell upon them to the exclusion of its orientalism. But the feudal lady was allowed to develop her mind. She was better educated than her husband. When circumstances made her a patron of literature, minnesong bloomed and the romance of chivalry. The orientalised lady of the South was discouraged from systematic education; in fact it was virtually impossible for her to get it. Her husband was far better educated than she. The literature produced to supply her demands was that of Mrs. Southworth and Miss Evans. It filled the planter with unfeigned horror to hear of the employment of women in the Northern states for useful purposes. Thomas Dabney was reduced to great poverty in his old age by his determination to pay debts incurred through the bad faith of another. The touching picture of the heroic old man and his daughters giving up such ease of life as the war had left them shows that some illusions had survived. His chivalrous nature (says his daughter) had always revolted from the sight of a woman doing hard work, and he could not have survived the knowledge that his daughters had stood at the washtub. So he did the washing himself, beginning in his seventieth year. So artfully is the human mind composed that he who had complacently employed women all his life to hoe his cotton without pay, could not stand the demolition of the lady. It remains to be said that it was not every planter whose orientalism was of so altogether lovable a type as Thomas Dabney's.

The Southern lady was forced by war and

ruin to make in a day the transition that the rest of the world had taken several centuries to effect. And she had to make it under the most disheartening conditions. In many cases she was mourning for a man who had died defending a cause of which no one but his fellows would take his point of view. It was plain that the men of the South would go down in history as having fought to retain an institution which the world at large had come to think altogether iniquitous. And they had been beaten. That the Southern lady should change her opinions was not to be expected; her mental training was not of a kind to make reasoning an easy or a familiar process. If she had been capable of changing her opinions she would have been all the time a different kind of woman and slavery would have come to an end long before. It was not then with the inspiration of an awakening but with the bitterness of uncomprehension, and therefore with all the more heroism, that after being so roughly tumbled from her high place she picked herself up and made herself useful. A Southern gentleman told Miss Martineau that nothing but the possession of genius or the arrival of calamity could rescue the lady of the plantation from her orientalism. What genius could at best have done but for an individual here and there, calamity did for a whole class.

As the calamity was unexampled, so was the response. It has perhaps not happened twice in history that so great a number of civilised women were reduced from comfort to misery in the same length of time as in the confederate states during the last two years of the Civil War. The courage of their men and their own courage served but to prolong the struggle and to deepen the misery. And the misery produced a type of heroism compounded of high spirit, endurance and efficiency, that the world has agreed to honour as one of the most stimulating and admirable achievements of the race.

THE END

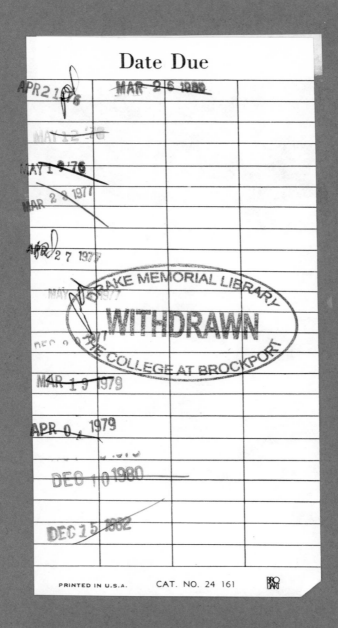